Psychoeducational Assessment
of Visually Impaired
and Blind Students

Psychoeducational Assessment of Visually Impaired and Blind Students

INFANCY THROUGH HIGH SCHOOL

Sharon Bradley-Johnson

5341 Industrial Oaks Boulevard
Austin, Texas 78735

Printed in the United States of America

Library of Congress Cataloging-in-Publication Data

Bradley-Johnson, Sharon.
   Psychoeducational assessment of visually impaired and blind students.

   Bibliography: p.
   Includes index.
   1. Children, Blind. 2 Visually impaired children. 3. Educational tests and measurements. 4. Psychological tests for children. I. Title. [DNLM: 1. Blindness–in adolescence. 2. Blindness–in infancy & childhood. 3. Educational Measurement. 4. Psychological Tests. 5. Vision Disorders in adolescence. HV 1598 B811p]
HV1596.2.B72 1986   371.91'1   85-23253
ISBN O-89079-108-2

5341 Industrial Oaks Boulevard
Austin, Texas 78735

10 9 8 7 6 5 4 3 2 1   86 87 88 89 90 91

Contents

Foreword

Reviewing material prior to publication can become uncomfortable when it seems that the material is too restrictive or that the opinions expressed are somewhat faulty. I am pleased to say that this book has neither of these flaws nor any other that I have discovered. I read this assessment guide with a great deal of interest, pleasure, and approval.

This is much more than a guide to assessing the visually impaired. For the evaluator, it gives a thorough evaluation of tools and methods which can be used to determine educational programs for visually impaired students. For the rest of us, it gives an overview of what constitutes a good approach with these same students and their parents. All who interact with the visually impaired could benefit from this book.

This approach has been needed for some time. While past attempts have been made to impart this information, none have included such a thorough, thoughtful treatment.

Bill J. Duckworth
Educational Research
American Printing House
for the Blind

Preface

Assessment of students who are not making adequate educational progress is difficult and time consuming. This task is even more challenging if the student has a physical handicap. Assessment results need to be educationally relevant, comprehensive, and obtained from tests and procedures that are reliable, valid, and appropriate for the student being tested. If these conditions are met, then the assessment results will contribute valuable information for developing programs that facilitate academic progress. However, if assessments are not carried out well, then use of inadequate results can further hinder the progress of students. For professionals whose charge it is to conduct psychoeducational assessments, this is a tremendous responsibility.

This book is primarily written to aid psychologists and educational consultants who are responsible for carrying out such assessments. The material is also useful to other professionals who must read assessment reports, participate in individualized educational planning meetings, and make decisions regarding educational programs for students.

To obtain useful assessment results the examiner must thoroughly understand the type of information that various tests and assessment procedures can provide as well as fully comprehend the limitations of the information that is obtained. Further, with students who have a physical impairment, one must be familiar with procedures that can circumvent a handicapping condition and understand how the handicap may affect a student's behavior. This is necessary to ensure that results accurately reflect a student's aptitudes and achievements. If these procedures are not employed, the results will describe only the limiting effect of the physical impairment on performance. In other words, the examiner should use psychoeducational tests for which the student is physically able to make the responses required (e.g., able to see items that require reading of print). This is both a legal (PL 93-112) and an ethical requirement.

Thus, in order to provide readers with sufficient information to meet the legal requirements and ethical responsibilities involved in assessing a student with a visual handicap, a general survey approach was avoided in presenting the material in this book. Instead, material is covered in a very detailed fashion. Moreover, the material is practice oriented.

The book is not intended to describe procedures for assessing visual impairment or blindness, because this is the responsibility of professionals in the medical field. Despite the fact that a number of visually impaired and blind children also have other handicaps, this book does not cover assessments of children who have multiple handicaps. These children have many special needs and the assessment process for them is very complex. Hence, they deserve an entire text specifically devoted to assessments that adequately meet their needs. The book also does not address vocational assessment; assessment of interests, skills, motivation, and personality traits relevant to job training is too extensive an area to include, and would require a separate text for sufficient coverage. Further, vocational assessment is relevant only for older students. However, the information this book provides on assessment of aptitudes and achievement describes important components of any assessment of vocational potential for students.

Contained in the book is: (a) material on procedures that can be used to obtain information during the process of assessment, (b) issues and background information relevant to assessment of students with little or no vision, (c) special procedures needed to obtain information on these students, and (d) detailed reviews of published, individually administered tests.

Specifically, Chapter 1 provides on overview of the assessment process. Chapter 2 presents background information useful in understanding the needs of these students and in interpreting their performance. In Chapter 3, special procedures used before and during assessment are described. These procedures are important in circumventing effects of visual impairment or blindness and obtaining valid results. Chapter 4 presents issues, assessment procedures, reviews of norm- and criterion-referenced tests, and reviews of informal measures for use with infants and preschoolers who have a visual loss. Chapter 5 covers these same topics as they relate to the school-aged child.

Acknowledgments

Preparation of any text is a lengthy and stressful endeavor that necessarily involves the efforts of numerous people. I am very grateful for the assistance I received. C. Merle Johnson offered many thoughtful comments, proofread material several times, and provided necessary encouragement. It was Jason Evans' keen sense of humor that allowed him to remain unscathed after frequent interruptions, but I appreciate the time he contributed while the material was being written. Bill Duckworth supplied important suggestions and invaluable support. Rosaleen Zoleski's patience, efficiency, and accurate typing of chaotic drafts was extremely valuable. Tracy Clapp cheerfully and competently typed in times of emergency. Finally, the editing and constructive criticism of Donald Hammill greatly improved the text.

Overview of
Assessment

In selecting instruments and procedures to assess the psychoeducational needs of a student, it is necessary to give considerable thought to the purposes for which the information will be used. Data from assessments can be used to make a variety of decisions; however, different decisions require different types of information. Because of the limited time available for assessments and the need for detailed, comprehensive information, organization of the assessment process is also critical. Before working with a student, an examiner must take into account the purposes of the assessment and how the assessment will proceed. The material that follows addresses the various purposes of assessment and the importance of sequence of procedures during the process of assessment.

Purposes of Assessment

Students are assessed for a number of reasons. One reason is screening to determine which students are at risk for delays in achievement and therefore require more individual attention. Once these students are identified, they are referred for more indepth assessment to determine their specific needs. Because a physical impairment is likely to significantly hamper a student's educational progress, it is usually not necessary to screen students with physical impairments to determine that they require special assistance.

Hammill (in press) has suggested other reasons for assessment: to diagnose students' problems, to identify instructional needs, to document progress in special programs, and to provide information for research. Because these are the primary purposes for assessing visually impaired and blind students, they are the focus of this text.

Diagnosis is not a listing of symptoms; rather, it is a theory to explain why the symptoms exist (Hammill, in press). A diagnosis is usually made by a multidisciplinary team and is based on data collected from a variety of sources. A diagnosis is not helpful in directly remediating problems; however, it can be helpful in determining whether or not the primary cause of the student's difficulty is physical impairment, or if another condition (e.g., mental retardation or learning disabilities) is the primary concern. If mental retardation or learning disabilities appears to be the primary problem, then the student will be eligible for special education services and programs beyond those available to students whose only diagnosis is visual impairment or blindness.

To make such a decision regarding eligibility requires a norm-referenced interpretation of data. This type of interpretation allows comparison of the student's performance with the performance of other students of the same age or grade level. PL 94-142 requires norm-referenced information to determine eligibility for special education services for those who are mentally retarded or learning disabled.

To identify a student's instructional needs is an equally important purpose of assessment. An assessment that does not result in improved academic performance by a student experiencing difficulty serves no useful purpose. The assessment process is a means to an end, not an end in itself (Ross, 1976).

The primary goal of assessment is to enable the student to learn more skills. In order to facilitate academic progress, it is necessary to determine a student's strengths as well as areas needing improvement. Both of these areas must be assessed in detail to identify specific skills for instruction. For example, a student's general area of difficulty could be reading braille, but the specific skills that need to be taught would be recognition of the letters *i, j, r,* and *s* and the phonograms *ble, ch, com,* and *con.* Another example is a student whose general area of strength is addition, and the specific skills that require instruction are double column addition with and without regrouping.

Norm-referenced information can be used to identify general areas of strength and difficulty. However, criterion-referenced information, data from systematic direct observation, and determination of problem solving strategies that the student uses are also necessary to identify specific instructional needs. All of these procedures are discussed in detail under The Process of Assessment.

To document progress in special programs and to provide information for research can require any or all of the types of information previously described. For example, both norm-referenced information and criterion-referenced information may be used to evaluate progress in a reading program for a student. If one purpose of a research project were to determine how improved academic performance affected behavior, then norm-referenced information might be used to document improvement in math and reading. Direct observation of behavior could be used to assess the frequency of certain behaviors of interest to the researchers.

The Process of Assessment

Assessment typically proceeds from the collection of general information about a student to the acquisition of data describing specific skills that have been learned as well as the next skills that are important to teach. The process can be viewed as a funnel, because information gathering proceeds through several stages from general to specific.

Administration of tests is only one element of the assessment process. Additional procedures that can be employed include interviews, review of school records, use of rating scales and checklists, and direct observation. The order in which these procedures are used will vary depending on the nature of the student's problem and the schedules of those involved in the assessment. However, the most efficient order is to employ procedures that yield general information first. These procedures include interviews, rating scales and checklists, and review of school records. Based on this information, the examiner can form hypotheses about the general nature of the problems and plan which specific assessment procedures to use to test these hypotheses. The procedures that would provide more specific information are direct observation and administration of norm- and criterion-referenced tests.

Interviews

The purpose of an interview is to obtain as much information as possible about a student's strengths or problem areas from the perspective of the student, the teacher(s), the parent(s), and relevant others familiar with the student's performance. Professionals other than the student's teacher can provide useful information which may differ from that given by the teacher. This is because other professionals, such as orientation and mobility instructors or speech therapists, interact with the student in settings other than the classroom and in situations with different requirements. For visually impaired and blind students, it is particularly important to obtain interview information from several sources because the limitations of the visual handicap are likely to vary as a function of the requirements of a particular situation. Information from various sources can be useful in planning educational programs. For example, the information given by an orientation and mobility instructor who has observed the student's use of right and left orientation in both indoor and outdoor environments, on and off school grounds, may be different from information given by the teacher. The teacher may have observed the student's use of right and left orientation only on school grounds and while the teacher was attending to several other behaviors at the same time.

Obtaining the student's opinion regarding his or her performance can also provide important information for program planning. For example, if a student's academic performance is poor, yet she or he does not feel that this is a serious problem, this suggests that the examiner and teacher will have to consider motivational problems as well as academic issues if performance is to be improved.

When assessment involves infants or preschoolers, more information usually can be obtained from an interview conducted in the home rather than in a school or office setting. The home environment allows the examiner an opportunity to observe the interaction of the parent(s) and child in a familiar setting. For a visually impaired or blind child, there are numerous behaviors requiring information from the parents' perspective which are not as critical for sighted children. Information on these behaviors can be used to suggest to parents things they can do to prevent or reduce delays in development that frequently occur in visually handicapped children. The Checklist for Home Observation of Visually Impaired and Blind Infants and Preschoolers in Table 1 is designed to aid examiners in an interview and in observation done in the home. Many items on the checklist can also be used with preschool teachers if the child is enrolled in a preschool program. Following Table 1 is a rationale for each of the items. The items are to be used as a guide for questions during the interview. It is best to ask the questions using an open ended format rather than one that suggests a "yes" or "no" response. For example,

TABLE 1
Checklist for Home Observation of Visually Impaired and Blind Infants and Preschoolers

Child

1. Other than making vocal sounds, does the child initiate interaction with the environment (i.e., child is active rather than passive)?	yes	no	not applicable
2. What type of nonvocal messages does the child use in response to others (e.g., quieting, squirming)?			
3. If child is mobile, does he or she seem to be aware of hazards and try to avoid them and/ or respond appropriately to "no-no"?	yes	no	not applicable
4. Does the child search for lost or dropped objects?	yes	no	not applicable

Parents

5. Does the child receive plenty of physical contact (e.g., being held, cuddled, touched)?	yes	no	
6. Do parents encourage the child to use hands to explore objects?	yes	no	
7. Is the child encouraged or prompted to move?	yes	no	not necessary because child moves frequently
8. Is the infant's position changed when he or she is lying down (e.g., back, tummy, side)?	yes	no	not applicable
9. Do parents frequently name objects and actions for the child?	yes	no	
10. Do parents often use the child's name before saying something to the child?	yes	no	
11. Does the child seem to be over-protected to the point it seriously limits interaction with the environment?	yes	no	not applicable

Home

12. Does the child have a specific place for storing toys?	yes	no	not applicable
13. Is the house reasonably uncluttered and organized so that the child can move about without tripping on things or running into objects unnecessarily?	yes	no	not applicable

Permission is given by the publisher to reproduce this checklist.

item 4 could be asked by saying, "What does your child do when she loses or drops an object?" An open ended format is likely to result in more accurate information, while questions that request a "yes" or "no" answer are more likely to result in answers that the parent considers socially acceptable. The checklist items are also useful for observation of the child in the home. (See the Direct Observation section in this chapter.)

The rationale for each of the checklist items follows.

1. Blind children and visually impaired children may become passive because the visual input is not available to entice them to reach out and interact with their environment. These children are often delayed in motor skills and self-initiated sensorimotor abilities (Fewell, 1983). Hence, it is worth noting whether the child uses self-initiated motor behaviors, other than vocal responses, to interact with objects in the environment. These behaviors could include such things as reaching for a cookie or bottle, searching for a fallen toy, or kicking or hitting a musical roly-poly toy. "Not applicable" is used for young infants who may move very little.

2. When parents talk to their infant who has a severe loss of vision, they may be disappointed and even feel rejected because the baby does not make eye contact nor orient toward their faces. If they do not find it reinforcing to interact with their baby, their attempts to communicate will decrease. Thus, parents can benefit from learning what behaviors to look for that indicate that their baby is responding in some way to their attention. The examiner may wish to explain to the parents that lack of eye contact does not mean the baby is not cognizant of their presence. It will be helpful to then make the parents aware of what other behaviors indicate that the baby is responding to them. These behaviors will include any rather consistent change in responding following an interaction with the parent. For example: quieting (i.e., slowing down movement or holding still), increase in activity (i.e., kicking, waving the arms, squirming), change in facial expression, or change in breathing rate. The parents' positive interaction with the baby is critical for the infant's optimal development.

3. As mentioned earlier, safety is a primary concern. The sooner children learn to protect themselves from danger, the better. Parents cannot always be there when a child needs protection or may not be able to get to a child soon enough to prevent an accident. Knowing to stop an activity in response to "no-no" could prevent a serious injury. "Not applicable" is used if the child is not independently mobile.

4. It is more difficult for a child with a severe visual loss to learn that if a toy is dropped or misplaced, it still exists and can be regained if the child searches for it (i.e., object permanence). To some infants, it is as if a dropped or misplaced toy falls into an abyss and no longer exists; this can cause frustration or passivity. These infants need to be physically

prompted to search for and find dropped or misplaced objects. "Not applicable" is used for babies who.are too young to demonstrate this behavior.

5. Children learn a great deal through physical contact, especially children with a visual loss. Physical contact can facilitate development in terms of cognition, socialization, language, and motor skills. Visually impaired and blind children need additional stimulation from being held and caressed by their parents. When a child has learned to find physical contact pleasurable it will help prevent isolation and passivity.

6. Infants and toddlers with a severe visual loss will have to learn a lot about the environment through touch. The sooner a baby begins to use touch, the sooner he or she can obtain information via this modality. Very early on parents can physically prompt their baby to explore objects using touch whenever possible.

7. Children with a severe visual loss tend to have delays in motor development; hence, they need a good deal of stimulation to move about in an attempt to prevent these delays. Without the visual stimulation to entice them to interact with their surroundings, they are more apt to be passive than sighted children. Briefly exercising the baby and physically prompting him or her to move will encourage more activity. If the child moves independently, circle "not necessary because child moves frequently."

8. If a visually impaired or blind infant is always allowed to remain in one position when lying down (e.g., supine) he or she may become content to remain in that position. Babies that have been hospitalized for lengthy periods may have been kept on their backs. To ensure that a baby uses different muscle systems (especially the upper extremities) and does not become passive, the baby's position will need to be changed, even if he or she does not enjoy being in the prone position. "Not applicable" is used if the baby is independently mobile.

9. More exposure to language is necessary for children with visual loss because they do not have the visual input of sighted children to aid in concept development. Parents can help by frequently naming objects and describing actions, even for infants.

10. If the child's name is used before something else is said it will serve two purposes. It will help the child learn his or her name and will let the child know that what is about to be said is directed to him or her. This is a useful habit for parents to establish for themselves.

11. As noted earlier safety is a primary concern, but interaction with the environment is also important to reduce passivity and withdrawal. "Not applicable" is used for babies who are not independently mobile.

12. If toys are kept in one place the child will know where to find them on his or her own. When the child is encouraged to put the toys away in the same spot, this teaches the importance of order and neatness which will be of great benefit later on as well. The child who is orderly

has greater control and independence. Parents can begin to teach this even to young children. "Not applicable" is used if the baby is not independently mobile.

13. If the house is reasonably uncluttered and things are kept pretty much in the same place, it will be easier for the child to learn to navigate and to be less fearful and more willing to move about the house. "Not applicable" is used if the baby is not walking.

For the school-age child with a visual handicap, the interview with the teacher is a critical facet of assessment. The teacher's view of a child's strengths and difficulties, and what has been tried to remediate the difficulties, must be determined if intervention programs are to be effective. Further, an examiner needs to determine prior to testing what adaptive devices, special materials, and procedures are used in the classroom that might also be useful during testing. Thus, this interview will be more useful if it is conducted prior to the administration of tests to a student.

There are special concerns that need to be addressed in an interview with the teacher of visually impaired and blind students. Table 2, Teacher Interview/Classroom Observation Checklist for Visually Impaired and Blind Students, can be used as a guide for the examiner during the interview with the teacher to address those concerns. Use of the checklist during observation of the student is discussed later in the chapter under Direct Observation.

It is also helpful during the interview with the teacher to obtain samples of the student's work, especially for areas of difficulty. From an examination of these work samples one can often determine error patterns. A remedial program can then be designed to correct such error patterns.

If rating scales or checklists are to be completed by a teacher or a parent, it is helpful to have the forms filled out at the end of the interview. This way the examiner would be present to clarify any questions that a parent or teacher might have in completing the forms. Further, the examiner will be sure to have the information in hand prior to directly testing or observing the student.

One rating scale for students with a visual handicap that is designed to be completed by the teacher is the *Pupil Behavior Rating Scale* (Swallow, Mangold, & Mangold, 1978). The scale consists of 24 items dealing with auditory comprehension and listening, spoken language, orientation, behavior, and motor skills. Each item has five choices that range from superior performance to extremely poor performance. Though the information obtained is general, the results suggest areas that may need to be investigated further by direct observation or testing.

TABLE 2
Teacher Interview/Classroom Observation Checklist
for Visually Impaired and Blind Students

Does student:	Yes	No
1. Request help when needed?	___	___
2. Accept help courteously?	___	___
3. Refuse help courteously?	___	___
4. Display an appropriate degree of independence?	___	___
5. Listen well to instructions?	___	___
6. Move freely about the classroom?	___	___
7. Avoid hazards as much as possible?	___	___
8. Have desk well organized and free of unnecessary materials?	___	___
9. Put materials back in their appropriate places so they can be easily located?	___	___
10. Interact with peers about as often as other students?	___	___
11. Interact in a positive way with peers?	___	___
12. Handle difficult or frustrating tasks without becoming overly upset?	___	___
13. Respond to corrective feedback appropriately?	___	___
14. Seem to appreciate praise from the teacher? Examples of effective praise statements:	___	___

15. What type of instructional materials are used?

_____ braille   _____ talking books   _____ large print

_____ Optacon   _____ cassettes   _____ material read to

_____ computer   student

other _____

16. What low-vision aids are used? _____

17. What special writing materials are used?

_____ braille writer   _____ slate and stylus   other _____

_____ typewriter   _____ special paper

(embossed or bold line)

18. What special arithmetic aids are used?

_____ abacus   _____ computer aids

_____ talking calculator _____ braille ruler

_____ special paper   _____ special clock

(embossed or bold line) (braille or raised numbers)

19. How frequently does student need breaks due to fatigue?

TABLE 2 Continued

20. Approximately how much extra time does student require to complete asssignments?

_____

21. What, if any, special lighting is required for reading?

_____

22. About how far are materials held from eyes for reading?

_____

Permission is given by the publisher to reproduce this checklist.

Review of School Records

A review of school records is needed prior to direct observation and testing for two reasons: (a) in order to avoid repeating assessment procedures that have recently been used, and (b) to obtain additional information useful in planning observations and testing. A review of the files should result in organized, comprehensive, yet concise notes. If this is the case it should not be necessary to return to the files to obtain information needed for the report. It will be helpful to make note of the following information:

- dates and results of tests for hearing, speech, and medical problems
- dates and results of prior tests
- names and dates of schools previously attended
- relevant anecdotal teacher notes
- relevant family information such as the person with whom the child lives
- dates and notes regarding prior school contacts with the family

For visually impaired and blind students a careful examination of the report on the student's eye examination is necessary. The following information may help the examiner interpret the report.

Visual acuity refers to the clarity of vision. Vision is measured separately for both right and left eyes. Normal vision is described as 20/20 when measured in feet or 6/6 in meters. This information is obtained from testing with the Snellen Wall Chart. If a student's vision is described as

20/200 this means that the student is able to discriminate letters on the chart at 20 feet that someone with normal vision could discriminate at 200 feet.

In addition to information on visual acuity, a report from an ophthalmologist typically will describe the etiology of the visual loss. There are numerous conditions that can result in loss of vision. Examples include retinitis pigmentosa (an inherited condition), cataracts (due to heredity, disease, or accidents), and optic nerve atrophy (damage to some or all of the nerve fibers).

If a student's visual loss is described as *congenital*, this means the child was born with this problem. If the visual loss is characterized as *adventitious*, it was a result of an accident or disease.

If a child has some usable vision, it is especially important to note the description of the student's field of vision. For example, if a student has only peripheral vision, he or she will have to fixate off center on objects to use this vision. If the student has a restricted visual field, but central vision, he or she will be able to look directly at an object to see it, but will be able to see only a small portion of that object near the center of fixation.

Usually the report will also indicate whether the loss occurred gradually or suddenly and whether the condition is stable, progressively deteriorating, or can be improved. This information is critical for planning educational programs. The ophthalmologist will make recommendations for medical intervention, prescriptions, and restrictions on use of the eyes if needed.

Observation

Direct observation of a student's performance is an integral part of any educational assessment for a visually impaired or blind student. Observation in the classroom environment is needed to plan a realistic educational program. However, observation in the home setting is also likely to provide useful information which is different from that obtained in the classroom. Because the home situation is more familiar, and parents may have expectations for the student that are not the same as those of school personnel, it is well worthwhile to observe the student in his or her home environment. For example, a visually impaired or blind student's willingness and ability to independently travel about the home may be quite different from his or her willingness or ability to travel about the classroom. Comparing information from observation in both settings could help determine how the classroom environment could be changed to facilitate the student's independence.

Observation of a student in the classroom prior to testing allows an examiner to become familiar with the student's needs and behaviors. This information is useful for selecting any special materials, procedures, or devices that would help achieve maximum performance during testing. For example, through observation an examiner might determine that special lighting is needed or determine what activities would be useful to establish rapport. Observation is especially important for examiners who have limited experience in assessing visually impaired or blind students because it will help them know what to expect during testing. This information should strengthen an examiner's confidence and help him or her to relax so that more attention can be paid to the student during testing.

Information obtained by an examiner observing in the classroom provides an objective perspective on the student's performance. Though information obtained by interviewing the teacher is obviously important, there are many reasons why it may not be entirely accurate. For example, a teacher may describe a student's performance as better than it actually is to prevent the student from being removed from the regular classroom to a special education classroom. If a teacher is unaccustomed to working with visually handicapped students she or he may not understand their special needs (e.g., more frequent breaks due to fatigue). This lack of understanding could cause unnecessary problems and an inaccurate assessment of a student's abilities. Hence, direct observation of a student in the classroom provides an additional perspective on the student's performance.

A good way to begin classroom observation is by using items from the Teacher Interview/Classroom Observation Checklist for Visually Impaired and Blind Students (Table 2). These items show things to look for during initial observation.

The Checklist for Home Observation of Visually Impaired and Blind Infants and Preschoolers (Table 1) is a useful place to begin observation of young visually impaired or blind children. This information will serve as a check on the reliability of the information obtained from parents. Items from this checklist can also be used to observe children enrolled in a preschool program. If the checklist is used at home and in the preschool, behavior in both settings can be compared. Comparisons can also be made of input from parents, teachers, and observations made by the examiner.

If problem behaviors are noted during interviews, on rating scales or checklists, or during observation using items from the checklists mentioned above, then a more detailed and systematic form of direct observation will be necessary. Fortunately, the procedures for carrying out direct observation are no different for visually impaired or blind children than for sighted children. However, in some cases the behaviors that are of concern will be different. For example, eye pressing is a problem behavior observed somewhat frequently in visually impaired or blind children and rarely seen in sighted children. (Eye pressing is discussed in more detail in Chapter 3.) If eye pressing were a behavior of concern to a teacher, interval recording would be a viable method of systematic direct observation to use to assess the problem. An example of assessment results obtained through systematic direct observation follows:

Susan was observed in three school situations: a very structured reading group, a semistructured reading group, and during an unstructured reading assignment to be done at her seat. Another girl considered to be "average" by the teacher was observed during these same times for comparison purposes. Every five minutes the entire class was scanned and any eye pressing recorded to provide additional comparative data with her peers. A 15-second interval procedure was used for observation. Data were collected on the number of intervals during which eye pressing was observed.

1. Structured Reading Session (15 mins/60 intervals)

Susan	Comparison Student	Class (3 scans)
1	0	0%

2. Semistructured Reading Session (15 mins/60 intervals)

Susan	Comparison Student	Class (3 scans)
2	0	0%

3. Unstructured Reading Seatwork (15 mins/60 intervals)

Susan	Comparison Student	Class (3 scans)
31	0	0%

In summary, Susan rarely engages in eye pressing in structured or semistructured situations. Her classmates do not demonstrate this behavior. However, in unstructured situations Susan frequently engages in eye pressing. From this information it is apparent that to decrease eye pressing it will be necessary to praise Susan whenever she does not engage in eye pressing in unstructured situations. It will also help to teach her relaxation behaviors incompatible with eye pressing to use in these situations, and to gradually increase the time she works on tasks that are unstructured.

Whether data from systematic behavior observation are accurate depends on the training and experience of the examiner. Several excellent resources describe procedures for the systematic observation of behavior (e.g., Alessi & Kaye, 1983; Gelfand & Hartman, 1984; Hall, 1983). A videotape which provides examiners with practice and feedback for recording accompanies the Alessi and Kaye text. All of these books also describe procedures for determining the reliability of the data, which is necessary if results are to be accurately interpreted.

Videotape may be helpful for observing and recording behavior in some situations, and is particularly useful for research projects and in evaluating the effect of intervention procedures.

Testing

Norm-referenced information from tests is necessary to determine eligibility for special education services. Tests used for this purpose must be technically adequate to insure that the normative group was an appropriate comparison for the particular student who was tested. The following criteria are useful in evaluating the technical adequacy of norm-referenced tests:

Standardization. Demographic data are needed to show that the sample corresponds to U.S. census data in terms of sex, race, socioeconomic level, geographic distribution, and urban-rural residence. Approximately 100 subjects are needed per age or grade level (Salvia & Ysseldyke, 1981).

Reliability. Test-retest data are needed by age or grade level. Correlations of .85 or better are needed with a two-week interval. Internal consistency and interrater reliability coefficients of this magnitude would be appropriate. Standard errors of measurement should be provided by age or grade level.

Validity. It is difficult to specify criteria for validity which is typically evaluated based on various types of research. A manual should provide a clear description of the rationale for item selection to assure the examiner of the content validity of a test. Information should also be provided on item analyses, item difficulty, criterion-related validity and construct validity. For a discussion of these concepts see Salvia & Ysseldyke (1981).

It may occasionally be necessary to use tests or parts of tests that do not meet minimum criteria for technical adequacy, such as when testing students with visual handicaps who also have other physical or mental handicaps which make it difficult for them to respond to test items. In this case, results must be interpreted with a great deal of caution, and as many data as possible need to be obtained from a variety of sources. Another reason data from less-than-adequate measures sometimes may be used is that the choices of tests for visually impaired or blind students are fewer than for sighted students. Fortunately, this situation is gradually improving as more technically adequate measures appear on the market.

Whether to use test norms for sighted students or for visually impaired and blind students is a question for which there is no simple answer. The examiner will need to consider the purpose for testing and the background of the student. If the purpose is to compare the student's current level of performance to that of sighted students in a regular classroom, and if the student is able to make the responses required by the test without difficulty, then norms for sighted students might be considered. However, in using these norms it is assumed that acculturation of the student has been similar to that of the sighted students in the norm sample. But this obviously is not the case, because the experiences the student has had are different. For example, the student may have been overprotected because of the visual impairment or blindness and thus have had limited experience interacting with the environment. If the student attended a residential school for visually impaired and blind students, his or her educational experience would be different from that of the norm group. Also, the student's life experiences would have been different because of little or no vision. Thus, as Salvia and Ysseldyke (1981) suggest, "...the norm comparisons are unfair" (p. 279). Keep in mind also that the content of these tests may not be appropriate for visually impaired and blind students because they have learning styles that are different from those of sighted students. Further, if because of the visual limitation the student is unable to respond to some of the items, adaptations would be necessary to circumvent the student's impairment. This would change the standardized administration procedures, and the comparison with the norms may not be appropriate. If the purpose is to use the information for planning an educational program, then adaptations and additional explanations would assist in determining strengths and difficulties.

Tests standardized on visually impaired and blind students are not without problems either. There are only a few available, and many of these have problems with different aspects of their technical adequacy. However, the requirements for responding to items will be more appropriate, and the normative sample may be more appropriate. The population of students with some type of visual impairment is very heterogenous. Age of onset of the visual impairment or blindness, whether gradual or sudden, and whether the student attended public or residential schools are examples of factors that cause considerable individual variation within this population. Hence, it is important that a relatively large and representative sample of visually impaired and blind students participate in the standardization of these tests to avoid biasing the norms.

Results of tests normed on students with little or no vision or for sighted students have problems with interpretation. Conclusions regarding educational programming and special education placement decisions need to be based on data from other sources of information as well. To determine the validity of standardized test results for a particular student, it will be necessary to examine their agreement with information obtained through interviews with several people who know the student well, data from criterion-referenced tests, and data from extensive classroom and home observation. (These procedures and tests are described in detail later in the book.) Further, an assessment that considers areas such as cognitive performance, academic performance, and adaptive behavior will be required to draw valid conclusions about a student's abilities. Periodic reevaluation will help determine the validity of prior test results as well as provide data on changes in the student's performance.

If it is possible to obtain data from tests standardized on sighted students, and from tests standardized on visually impaired and blind students, this will be beneficial. When these two sources of information are combined with information from interviews, criterion-referenced tests, and classroom as well as home observation, and if comprehensive and periodic assessments are carried out, a good information base will be available from which to draw conclusions.

If data from norm-referenced tests, interviews, or observation suggest that there are academic areas where the student is having difficulty, further testing with criterion-referenced tests is likely to be needed.

Results from criterion-referenced tests are not used to compare a student's performance to the performance of others. Instead, performance is assessed in terms of whether a student is able to perform a certain task to a preset level of mastery (i.e., a student passes or fails an item depending upon whether she or he reaches a certain criterion). For example, a mastery level for a skill might be that two out of three times the student correctly recognizes the short vowel sound for *u* in consonant-vowel-consonant words. Items on criterion-referenced tests are based on a detailed task analysis of skills, they assess more skills than norm-referenced tests, and each skill is usually tested two or three times. It is this specificity that is critical for planning instructional programs.

Criterion-referenced tests have an advantage over norm-referenced tests for visually impaired or blind children because various objects and materials can be used to assess skills. Use of adapted materials can aid in determining what these children are capable of doing (e.g., braille materials, larger toys, and black-light toys). Further, because the tests are not standardized, flexible administration procedures can be used. This flexibility can help to determine the most appropriate procedures for teaching a skill to a particular child.

For published criterion-referenced tests for infants and preschoolers, age levels are assigned to items. These age levels are typically based on literature reviews. Because the tests are not standardized, the age levels cannot be used as normed scores. The age levels only suggest the appropriate age at which children typically demonstrate the skills. In workshops on the *Diagnostic Inventory of Early Development* (Brigance, 1978), the following points are made: Published norms do not agree, norms change as prenatal care improves, developmental patterns are highly individual in infancy, and norms vary as a function of environmental and cultural differences. When testing visually impaired or blind children, the examiner must keep in mind that these approximate levels are based on the ages at which sighted children usually learn these skills. Generally, development of visually impaired or blind children follows the same pattern as that of sighted children, but it often proceeds at a slower rate. Thus, consideration needs to be given to those skills that usually require more time to learn for visually impaired and blind children. (See Chapter 4.)

In addition to criterion-referenced tests, a determination of the types of strategies students use to solve problems can be made (Hammill, in press). If a teacher is aware that the strategy a student is using is incorrect, then it is relatively easy to provide the student with one that works (Hammill, in press). For many problems there is more than one strategy that will enable a student to arrive at a correct answer. Examples of individual-referenced interpretation follow. Each of these strategies makes the student's performance inefficient.

Jackie uses her fingers to count when completing addition problems for sums greater than 10. (Hence, Jackie needs to learn these math facts.)

Jeremy comprehends better when reading braille if he whispers words as he reads. (Jeremy would benefit from learning to read without whispering.)

Various procedures including interviews, rating scales and checklists, review of school records, observation, and testing are needed to move from general information to the specification of the exact nature of a student's academic problems. There are important differences in each of these procedures when assessment of a visually impaired or blind child is involved rather than a sighted child. In order to carry out a comprehensive assessment, it is likely that norm-, criterion-, and individual-referenced information will be necessary.

Limitations of Assessment

The educational assessment of visually impaired and blind students is a time-consuming process. Despite the limitations in current assessment instruments, in most cases it is possible to obtain a considerable amount of norm-referenced information and detailed information needed for program planning. It is well worth the time required to obtain this information in order to make accurate decisions regarding special education placement. Detailed, comprehensive information is also necessary to plan effective educational programs for students.

Interviews with teachers, parents, and students are rich sources of information. Systematic observation of the student's performance in various settings is critical.

The type of assessment instruments described in the following chapters will yield many benefits to the assessment of visually handicapped students. A major problem in the assessment of visually impaired and blind students, however, is that nearly all tests designed for this population fail to meet minimum standards for technically adequate measures. While many tests developed for sighted students are technically adequate, these tests contain items or subtests that are inappropriate for students with little or no vision. The technical adequacy of tests for sighted students has improved dramatically in recent years. Authors of new tests for visually impaired and blind students could make a major contribution to the field if tests could be developed for these students that are well-standardized and have good reliability (especially test-retest data) and validity (particularly content validity).

More research is obviously necessary in the assessment of visually impaired and blind students. Specifically, new tests are needed (especially for cognitive assessment and achievement) that have norms for both sighted students and visually impaired and blind students. However, the tests that have the greatest potential for assisting in the education of these students are criterion-referenced tests. Any progress in this area would be an important advance in the field of education of visually impaired and blind students.

2

Critical Issues in Understanding Visually Impaired and Blind Children

To obtain valid test results, accurately interpret children's performance, and provide useful information for educational planning, examiners need to understand a number of issues related to visually impaired and blind children. A discussion of these issues is presented in this chapter: types of vision loss, incidence, the importance of useful vision, age effects for onset of vision loss, the need for periodic assessment of vision and hearing, medication considerations, assessment of orientation and mobility skills, behaviors affecting social interaction, concept development for these children, and issues in working with parents.

Visual Problems

A person is considered "legally blind" when central visual acuity is not more than 20/200 best corrected vision in the better eye or where the field of vision is limited to a diameter of no more than 20 degrees. These students will need to use senses other than vision in the educational process (Scholl, 1983).

Few people are totally blind; rather, most are able to perceive light and/or details to some degree. Over 75% of blind people in the United States have some usable vision (American Foundation for the Blind, undated).

For educational purposes, visual impairment can be considered mild, moderate, or severe (Scholl, 1983). Mild impairment refers to visual problems typically correctable with glasses. Students with moderate visual impairments learn mainly through sight, but need some type of modification of instructional materials. Those students with severe visual impairments must use senses other than vision in the educational process.

In this text, the term *blind* refers to those children with complete loss of sight. *Visually impaired* is applied to those students with more than mild visual impairments, but it does not include blind students. These visually impaired students have some degree of vision that in most cases can be used in the educational process. It is these two groups of students (blind and visually impaired needing more than glasses to function adequately in the classroom) who need some modification of procedures and/or materials in the assessment process.

There are approximately 6.4 million people in the United States who have difficulty seeing even when using corrective lenses. Because the main cause of blindness in the U.S. is associated with aging, about 65% of severely visually impaired persons are over 65 (American Foundation for the Blind, undated).

According to the Federal Quota Registration for the American Printing House for the Blind (1984), 44,313 students were registered. Of these students, 12,839 attended schools for the blind and 31,474 attended programs funded by state departments of education. There were 4,262 registered for infant and preschool programs; 774 children attended infant and preschool programs at schools for the blind; and 3,488 attended programs funded by state departments of education.

There are few visually impaired children who have no usable vision; many are able to read large or even regular print. Extended observation in the classroom and a teacher interview are necessary to determine how a child uses this vision. Two children with the same visual acuity are likely to differ a great deal in ability to use their vision. To assess use of vision on an informal basis, it is helpful to note such behaviors as the distance objects or materials are held from the eyes, size of print that can be read, and how much detail is observed in pictures (Scholl & Schnur, 1975). This information is needed to select appropriate assessment instruments and to plan educational programs that make optimum use of vision. Figure 1 displays examples of various print sizes.

All other things being equal, the younger the age at which a child first has a visual impairment or becomes blind, the greater the negative impact on the child's development. If loss of vision occurs before age five, it is likely to seriously affect educational progress (Salvia & Ysseldyke, 1981). If a child has had vision for the first 5 years or longer, she or he will have visual memories that can aid in learning. On the other hand, children who have never been able to see must develop these concepts based entirely on input from their other senses. It is important to consider this factor when drawing conclusions about a child's performance and in planning the child's educational program. For example, a student may give a questionable response to a verbal item. When the examiner probes for further information, it may be clear that the student has an incomplete understanding of the concept. The lack of a visual image may at least partially explain the incomplete answer. The question then becomes how to circumvent the lack of a visual image to help the student acquire a more complete understanding of the concept.

Sensory Functioning

For visually impaired students, optical aids and a particular size of print may be recommended. Eye conditions may change periodically and require changes in these recommendations. Hence, when observing the student in the classroom and during testing it should be noted how well the aids and print size the student is using appear to work. If after obtaining the teacher's, parent's, and student's opinions, there appears to be a problem, it would be appropriate to refer the student for a reevaluation of these aids and materials.

Because visually impaired and blind children must rely so heavily on auditory input, it is critical that periodic hearing assessments be made. Some types of hearing problems may occur on an intermittent basis, and these difficulties can be missed on a screening test. Thus, periodic comprehensive hearing examinations are good insurance against hearing problems that might further interfere with development of visually impaired and blind children.

Visually impaired and blind students are not more sensitive than sighted students in terms of their ability to discriminate using hearing,

Print Size 30

Walking in the woods, Alison heard a strange noise. ''Could it be an animal?'' Alison thought as she carefully looked around. Alison liked animals.

Print Size 22

Walking in the woods, Alison heard a strange noise. ''Could it be an animal?'' Alison thought as she carefully looked around. Alison liked animals.

Print Size 12

Walking in the woods, Alison heard a strange noise. ''Could it be an animal?'' Alison thought as she carefully looked around. Alison liked animals.

Figure 1.   Various print sizes.

taste, touch, and smell. Instead, they attend better when receiving information via these senses and thus are better able to interpret this information.

Medication Effects

Medication may affect behavior. For example, alertness, willingness to perform, and activity level may be enhanced or depressed. As much information as possible should be obtained from the teacher and parents regarding how the medication seems to affect the student's performance. It may be necessary to discuss the effects of the medication with the physician also. Further, it will be helpful to observe performance just before the medication is taken and again about an hour later to determine whether any behaviors change. If changes are evident, testing should be scheduled for a time when medication effects are least likely to interfere with performance. If criterion-referenced tests are used, it may be helpful to assess skills with and without the medication.

Orientation and Mobility

Evaluation and training by a specialist in orientation and mobility is a very important aspect of a visually impaired or blind student's education. An orientation and mobility instructor has had specialized training for teaching visually impaired and blind students how to effectively and safely travel about the environment. Unfortunately, these services are not required in all states. Considering the handicap, a visually impaired or blind student's ability to move about the environment may seem quite good to someone not trained in orientation and mobility. However, a specialist may be able to make suggestions that could considerably increase the student's level of independent functioning.

Behaviors Affecting Social Interaction

When talking with someone, a sighted person will turn his or her face toward the speaker. For severely visually impaired or blind persons, this is something that usually must be taught. Orienting to the speaker may not be an easy thing to do, especially in a group of people where several speakers are talking simultaneously. If a student turns away when the examiner is speaking during an assessment, this does not necessarily mean that he or she is trying to avoid the situation or the examiner. Probably the student has not yet learned to orient to the speaker. If this is the case, it is an important behavior to note and to include in the Individualized Educational Plan as a skill to be taught. If the student does not learn this skill it could make social interactions with others unnecessarily difficult.

Examiners who have had limited experience with visually impaired and blind persons may find that it can be difficult to interpret the emotions of some of these students. Some students may never have seen others' use of gestures. Gestures are learned from observation of others modeling these behaviors. Hence, caution is needed in interpreting the emotional reactions of visually impaired and blind students. They may be experiencing feelings appropriate to a situation, but may not have learned to express these feelings through the usual gestures.

Certain mannerisms or forms of self-stimulation by these students may seem bizarre. It is not appropriate to refer to these behaviors as "blindisms." Everyone, whether sighted or not, when bored or under stress, will on occasion engage in some level of self-stimulation. For example, think of people sitting in cars while traffic is tied up. It is common to observe different types of self-stimulation such as pinching at finger nails, foot tapping, lip biting, and even rocking in this situation. It is not unusual for visually impaired or blind students to engage in self-stimulation, particularly when they are bored or stressed. However, the type of self-stimulation may not be as acceptable or may be at a more intense level than that used by sighted persons.

A type of self-stimulation often used especially by young children is eye pressing. As Scott, Jan, and Freeman (1985) noted, the behavior can begin around 12 months of age with frequent rubbing of the eyes, and by about 18 months it can progress to a well-established habit where the child presses the thumbs against the eyes. If continued this can result in deeply depressed eyes that are discolored with dark circles. The behavior makes the child look strange to others and is a difficult habit to eliminate (Scott et al., 1985).

Other types of self-stimulation that visually impaired and blind children might engage in are light gazing, head rolling, and waving or flicking fingers. These behaviors also make a child appear unusual to others.

If such behaviors are observed they should be targeted for remediation. The types of situations in which self-stimulation is likely to occur need to be identified. It may be necessary to teach the student other ways to handle stress or boredom in order to eliminate the behaviors.

Concept Development

The development of concepts is more difficult for a child with a visual impairment or who is blind than for a sighted child, particularly if the loss of vision occurred before the age of 5. These children may have to learn many concepts through language, because they cannot experience them through the other intact senses. This can result in the child acquiring only a limited meaning for certain words. For example, it is difficult to teach the concept *cow* to some visually impaired children or to a child who is blind. If you give the child a model of a cow to explore, this presents a restricted view of *cow*. Then if the child is encouraged to touch a real cow, she or he receives information about *cow* in parts. The child must then integrate the information received about the parts into a whole.

Higgins (1973) investigated blind and sighted children's use of (a) words that can be experienced and (b) abstract words. Based on this work, Higgins suggested that a blind child may use a word in what seems to be a meaningful way but that this does not guarantee consistent logical use of the word in other contexts. In other words, the child may have an incomplete understanding of the word, making it relatively useless for application in other situations.

The extent of differences in concept development between sighted children and visually impaired and blind children requires considerably more research. For example, though many studies have suggested that differences exist, Anderson and Olson (1981) found no significant differences in the verbal descriptions of common objects between sighted and congenitally blind children.

Hence, conclusions regarding results of verbal tests must be made with caution at this point. Sometimes a visually impaired or blind child may receive a great deal of reinforcement for rote memory of information. This can contribute to the development of prolonged echolalia, both immediate and delayed. To avoid overestimating a child's level of performance, it is important to probe questionable responses and to observe the child's verbal behavior in a variety of contexts. Results of tests based on verbal items only should be interpreted in light of observation of the child's performance on other tasks in the classroom and at home.

Parents

Assessment of a visually impaired or blind child necessitates involving the child's parents in the process. This may require helping them cope with their child's handicap, especially if they are new parents. They are likely to be very concerned, even frightened, about the responsibility of raising a visually impaired or blind child. This prospect is particularly difficult if they have not had much contact with handicapped people. Their concern is realistic because they will have to face some arduous demands as parents.

One way professionals can help parents is by discussing with them the shock, grief, anger, and resentment parents feel when first informed that their child is not perfect, but handicapped. Talking over these feelings and acknowledging that many parents of handicapped children feel this way can be helpful. The fact that most visually impaired and blind children grow up to be happy, productive adults needs to be emphasized. In the discussions it may be useful to invite other family members (e.g., siblings and grandparents) to participate if they will be involved with the child and could provide support to the parents. It is usually helpful to arrange for the family to talk with visually impaired or blind adults about their experiences. Also, arranging for the family to meet other parents in the area who have visually impaired or blind children is beneficial. A list of parent groups and local and state agencies concerned with visually impaired and blind children should be given to the parents as well.

Another way to assist parents is to ensure that they recognize they are an important part of the educational planning process. The message that they are competent to help make decisions regarding their child's education must be conveyed. This may help them cope with their child's visual problems by fostering a sense of control over the family's situation.

To involve the parents in the planning process, it is necessary to avoid educational and psychological jargon in reports and in discussing test results. Jargon interferes with communication, and can cause a parent to feel incompetent in understanding the material and to feel alienated from the process. The use of technical language has consistently been an obstacle to parents' satisfaction in communicating with professionals (Korch, Gozzi, & Frances, 1968).

It can be advantageous to give parents some suggestions for activities that can be done at home. These activities should be related to the test results so that parents understand the purpose. Activities should be explained clearly, should require minimal time to implement, and should consider the family's strengths and limitations. Self-help skills, play activities, and language are areas where family members can be particularly helpful in teaching the child.

Commenting on things parents have done already to help their child can strengthen their feelings of competence. Parents should be encouraged in activities such as taking their child to the physician, making an accurate observation of the child's skills, teaching the child self-feeding, or taking the time to come to the school to discuss results of an assessment. As Cruickshank (1980) noted, the attitude of the parents and the support they provide are critical to the adjustment of the child.

The home environment that the parents provide is obviously important for a child's normal development, but the importance of moving handicapped students into the mainstream of educational services is also well-established. This does not necessarily mean, however, that there is no need for residential facilities in the education of visually impaired and blind students. It would be unreasonably expensive for local school districts to have the range of specialized equipment (e.g., adapted computer equipment, the Optacon, and new devices to facilitate orientation and mobility) and the staff trained to use such equipment. Therefore, as Scholl (1983) suggests, at some point in the student's education the use of a residential facility may be beneficial. She recommends that placement be made for a specified purpose that is not available in the regular school setting, and that the stay need be for only a short period during the academic year or during the summer.

Special Procedures
for Assessment

It is not unusual for an examiner who has had little or no experience with visually impaired and blind persons to feel uncertain and anxious at the prospect of testing such a student. As Scholl and Schnur (1975) suggested, the best advice is to respond to the student as a person and to use common sense. They point out that if an examiner is uncertain of how to handle a situation, asking the student is likely to provide the answer. It also never hurts to ask a student if she or he needs help with something. Following are special procedures that if employed before and during testing will aid in obtaining valid results and in making the process go smoothly for both the student and the examiner. These procedures pertain to aptitude and achievement testing. The assessment of a student's affective behaviors is not addressed in this text. The issues involved in assessing personality factors for visually impaired and blind students are so involved that there is not room in a text such as this to adequately cover this area.

Before Testing

The assessment process for a visually impaired or blind student will require considerably more time than that required for a sighted student. Hence, it will be necessary to plan the schedule accordingly and not try to rush the process.

If the student is blind or severely visually impaired, when taking the student to the room for testing offer your arm to hold. If the student would like you to lead the way, she or he will take hold of your upper arm or elbow. Keep your arm close to your body. For young children, hold their hand or let them hold your wrist. Lead the way to the room, and *never* push the student. If you come to curbs or stairways, say so and indicate whether it is a step up or down.

When talking to the student, first use his or her name. Talk using a normal level of conversation. The fact that a student has a visual problem does not mean that there is also a hearing impairment. Even if there were, talking loudly would not be helpful. The examiner's typical manner of speaking will be appropriate. It is not necessary to avoid using terms like *see* or *look*. Blind people readily use these words in their speech and the conversation will be awkward if an examiner tries to avoid using them.

When arriving at the room for testing, the student will need time to become oriented by exploring the room and feeling objects. The examiner can physically guide or otherwise encourage the student to do this. It will be helpful if the examiner describes the room, arrangement of furniture, and the objects. If the student chooses to explore the room independently, it is important that all doors are either completely open or closed; a student could be injured by walking into a half open door. The same information that a sighted student obtains about the testing situation through sight will need to be conveyed to the visually impaired or blind student through auditory or tactile means.

The examiner can seat the student either by placing the student's hand on the back of the chair and allowing the student to seat himself or herself, or by positioning the student so that the side of his or her leg contacts the front of the chair.

Adequate rapport is necessary prior to any testing. For some students this may require an extra session or two where the purpose is simply for the examiner and student to get to know one another and to establish easy communication. The purpose of the testing should be clearly explained to help reduce stress. If visually impaired students are tense, this can negatively affect their ability to use their usable vision (e.g., as with nystagmus). A tense examiner is likely to miss important observations and have difficulty administering the tests.

In the testing room any flickering light or glare can interfere with the use of a student's available vision and may cause fatigue. Glare can be caused by laminated materials or if the student is seated facing a window. It is important that the room be adequately illuminated. While some students need lighting of rather high intensity, others may be light sensitive and need low intensity illumination (e.g., students who have albinism). The light source should come from the side of the more efficient eye. Use of a rheostat will be helpful in finding the most appropriate level of illumination.

The room should be free of extraneous auditory or visual distractions. Because a visually impaired or blind student relies so heavily upon auditory input, extraneous noise (e g., ticking of a clock) can be a problem.

Special Materials

If a student uses special equipment and/or materials to aid in reading and writing in the classroom, these should be used during testing. What is appropriate for a particular student can be determined by talking with the teacher and observing in the classroom. The equipment or materials that would be appropriate for use during testing depends on the types of responses required for the tests that will be administered. Examples of special materials and equipment that enable students with a visual impairment to read are large print and braille materials, the Optacon (a device that converts print to braille), and closed circuit TV that magnifies print on a screen. Hand-held magnifiers, stand magnifiers, or magnifying spectacles might be used with visually impaired students. Book stands reduce fatigue caused from bending over to read, and they free the student's hands to hold a magnifier. A felt tip pen, a braille writer, a braille slate and stylus, a typewriter, or paper with bold or raised lines aid students in writing their responses. Figure 2 displays a braille writer and Figure 3 displays a braille slate and stylus.

The use of a yellow plastic laminate over a white sheet is beneficial for some students because it can increase contrast and thus produce a sharper copy. Whether or not this is helpful will have to be decided on an individual basis, but it is worth a try.

If manipulable objects are used in testing, it is usually a good idea to keep them on a tray. The tray keeps the objects where the student can easily locate them and reduces the need to search for fallen objects. Sides of the tray should be about two inches or less for easy access, such as on the Work/Play tray available from the American Printing House for the Blind. Figure 4 shows this tray.

Figure 2.   Braille writer. (Courtesy the American Printing House for the Blind.)

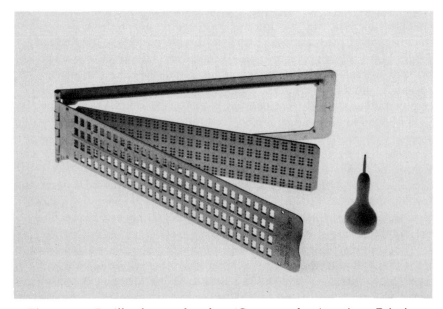

Figure 3.   Braille slate and stylus. (Courtesy the American Printing House for the Blind.)

Figure 4. Work/play tray. (Courtesy the American Printing House for the Blind.)

During Testing

Test taking can be an anxiety provoking situation, especially for a visually impaired or blind student. It can help reduce this anxiety and enable the student to understand what is taking place if the examiner describes what she or he is doing. For example, the examiner can indicate when she or he is putting materials away or taking them out, or can describe the fact that she or he is recording answers given by the student. The student will be guided through the assessment and will not have to guess about what is taking place.

A blind student, and many visually impaired students, cannot see an object or material when an examiner is handing it to them. Thus, it is helpful if the examiner touches the student's hand with the object or places the student's hand on the material to identify its location. Explain that you are handing him or her an object so as to avoid startling the student when the object touches the hand.

If a student drops an object, allow him or her to pick it up. It will be helpful if the examiner provides verbal rather than physical guidance. Directions given to the student must be specific. For example, "To your left" would be a functional direction for a blind student, while "Put it here" or "That way" would be meaningless.

Sighted students require discipline on occasion during testing and so will visually impaired students and blind students. The same standards for acceptable behavior need to be applied. It is not to the benefit of the student to do otherwise because if inappropriate behavior is allowed, it will negatively affect performance.

Details regarding test selection are given later in the book. However, several general issues are appropriate to discuss here. First, examiners need to be very familiar with the tests they will be using. If not, errors in administration are likely to be made and important observations of the student may be missed while searching through the manual for directions. If a selected test is one which the examiner has not previously administered, it would be a good idea to give it to sighted children first. This will give the examiner a reference for how sighted children perform on the test and will serve as a reminder of the range of individual differences in performance of sighted children as well. Second, tests with time limits penalize visually impaired and blind students for several reasons: (a) braille and large print take considerably longer to read and (b) manipulable objects require more time to locate and interpret when it is primarily the tactile sense that is used. If possible, it is better to avoid timed tests.

Because visually impaired and blind students are unable to see smiles and facial cues well, it is necessary for the examiner to convey approval of the student's performance through what is said and the tone of voice. This often requires a conscious effort by the examiner. Physical contact, such as a pat on the shoulder, can also enhance a student's motivation to perform well.

Fatigue is another factor that can substantially interfere with the performance of visually impaired students. Eye strain and general fatigue from employing usable vision are likely to occur. Blind students are also apt to become fatigued before a test is completed because of the length of time it takes to read braille. Thus, it is possible that several sessions may be needed to administer each test. Discontinue testing if fatigue is noted.

Assessment of visually impaired and blind students necessarily will be time consuming and sometimes difficult. However, these efforts are worthwhile because they enable the examiner to make valid judgments regarding the most appropriate educational program for a student.

Assessment of Infants and Preschoolers

Typically, assessment of an infant or preschooler is more difficult than assessment of a school-aged child. One reason for this is the large number of considerations involved (e.g., preambulatory skills, response to objects, self-help skills, and prelanguage skills). This necessarily makes an assessment time consuming, and infants and preschoolers are rarely patient with the activities over extended time periods. Second, infants and many preschoolers will not demonstrate a skill upon the request of an examiner, so a great deal of information must be obtained from observation of the infant's or preschooler's spontaneous behavior during the testing session. So that the demonstration of important skills is not missed, an examiner must know what to look for and must be a conscientious observer. Finally, it is important to involve the parents as part of the assessment process, because they will be needed to help carry out intervention plans. Thus, considerable expertise in assessment of infants and preschoolers as well as good interpersonal skills are necessary. In addition, knowledge of issues specific to these young children who have a visual loss is critical. A discussion of these issues is presented in this chapter, along with a description of special considerations for assessment, and detailed reviews of norm- and criterion-referenced tests and informal measures.

General Issues

Parents usually wonder what pattern and rate of development they can expect for their visually impaired or blind child. In general, these children progress through the same sequence of development as other children, but there may be delays in the emergence of some skills. (The specific areas that may be delayed are presented later in this chapter when the various areas to be assessed are discussed.) However, with good teaching some of these delays can be avoided or lessened. It should be kept in mind that even with sighted infants, there are considerable individual differences in the rate of development.

Because hearing is so important to the development of visually impaired and blind children, it is critical that a comprehensive hearing assessment be carried out. This can be done as early as the day a baby is born, so age is not a factor.

Some parents of handicapped children become so concerned about their child's safety that they are overly protective and thereby severely limit their child's interaction with the environment. Protecting the child from harm is critical, but the child will also need to learn self-protection by avoiding hazards. In addition, one ought not overlook the fact that visually impaired and blind children require as much contact with the environment as possible. Experiencing the environment through touching and exploring will facilitate cognitive development, independence, and curiosity.

Between the ages of 18 and 30 months some visually impaired children will engage in a behavior that appears to be unusual unless the reason for it is understood (Scott et al., 1985). If the child must hold things several inches from his or her eyes to see them, it can be tiring on the arms. Because the child's hip joints at this age are about at the midpoint of the body, some children may discover that it is possible to bend over and make a tripod by putting the head on the floor. Then if the forearms are placed on the floor, it is possible to examine objects that are held in the hands for rather lengthy periods as this is a comfortable position. When the child's legs grow longer, this behavior will disappear because it will not be possible to comfortably assume this position.

Sighted infants and young children are able to see when someone is going to pick them up. This is not the case for blind and severely visually impaired children. Thus, to avoid a startle response, speak first using the child's name before picking up the child.

Another thing to consider during testing and in making recommendations to the parents is that some young children with a visual impairment or who are blind do not like to touch fuzzy or furry toys. These toys seem to frighten them (Scott et al., 1985).

For children who have not been in an educational program outside the home, it is best to carry out the assessment in the home. This is the environment with which the child is most familiar and is where she or he will feel most comfortable. Parents will be more relaxed at home as well. If the child has participated in an educational program outside the home, then observations in both settings will be useful for comparison.

Special Assessment Issues

Cognitive Development

Presently there is no norm-referenced test of cognitive development that has been standardized on children under the age of 6 who have little or no vision. Further, norm-referenced tests standardized on sighted children under the age of 4 require vision on a number of items. It is not possible to adapt all of these items to circumvent limited vision or lack of vision. Because of these problems, it is impossible at this time to obtain a valid IQ score for children with little or no vision who are under 4 years of age.

The best alternative for these children seems to be to estimate a child's abilities by using age-referenced items from standardized tests that do not require vision, or that can be adequately adapted to circumvent visual requirements and still measure the same skills. Then results can be described as an age range of items that the child was able to successfully complete. This type of estimate can aid in understanding the child's current needs. An example of such a description follows.

Elizabeth was able to complete nearly all of the cognitive tasks that did not require vision and that are usually performed by children of approximately 13 months of age. Several items were adapted so that visual responses were not required, and feedback from sounds and touch was maximized for her. Adaptations included use of a larger set of pegs and pegboard so that Elizabeth was able to locate the items and insert the pegs. Also, blocks with bells in them were used when she was asked to put blocks in a cup.

Two published tests of cognitive development for children less than 4 years of age contain age-referenced items: the *Bayley Scales of Infant Development* (Bayley, 1969) and the *Battelle Developmental Inventory* (Newborg, Stock, Wnek, Guidabaldi, & Svinicki, 1984). Two other standardized tests with age-referenced items are currently being developed. *Cognitive Abilities Relevant to Education* (Bradley-Johnson, in press) will be for 2- and 3-year-old children. It has five sections: Early Reading, Early Arithmetic, Language, Handwriting, and Enabling Behaviors. The Fourth Edition of the *Stanford-Binet Intelligence Scale* (Thorndike, Hagen & Sattler, 1986) will have an age range from 2 years to superior adult. It will have scores for Verbal Reasoning, Quantitative Reasoning, Visual Spatial Reasoning, and Short Term Memory. These latter two tests will not be reviewed because the technical information is not yet available. All four of these tests have some items that require vision and many that do not. Adaptations could be made to circumvent visual problems for some items.

Because of the limitations of using age-referenced items when overall scores cannot be determined, the data would require cautious interpretation. Results would need to be described, along with information on other areas of development obtained from other tests, and with observational and interview data.

For children who are 4 years old and older, there are other tests available to assess cognitive development. It is possible to obtain a valid score in this area for most children with little or no vision who are at least 4 years old.

Motor Development

Both fine and gross motor development tend to be delayed for infants and preschoolers who are visually impaired or blind. However, there can be a great deal of individual variability in motor skill development, as there is for sighted children. The child's experiences can play a major role in either facilitating or inhibiting the development of motor skills. For example, if an infant has been hospitalized for a period of time and kept on his or her back, the baby's muscle tone is likely to be poor. The limited opportunity to practice moving will delay motor development. Also, because a child with little or no vision is not enticed by visual stimulation from the environment, she or he may become passive. If a caregiver stimulates a child with sound producing toys and physically prompts the child to engage in behaviors such as crawling and walking, few if any delays may be evident.

In carrying out an assessment of motor development, an examiner will need to consider that it is not unusual for a child with a visual impairment or who is blind to take longer to develop some motor skills because of the vision problem. This does not mean that all children with serious visual problems will be delayed in these areas; many delays can be prevented. However, a visual impairment or blindness does make it more difficult to learn the following skills.

Motor Skills Often Delayed. Skills usually learned by sighted babies between approximately birth and 1 year of age that may require more time for a child with little or no vision to learn are:

- turning to sound
- reaching for toys that make sounds
- lifting head and chest when on stomach
- holding head erect
- turning over
- pulling self to a standing position
- crawling

Skills usually learned by sighted babies between approximately 1 and 2 years of age that may require more time to learn are:

- walking (Most blind children walk by about 20 months of age, Scott et al., 1985.)
- turning book pages
- use of pull toys
- rolling and catching patterned, brightly colored balls or a ball with a beeper
- fine motor skills

According to *The Oregon Project* (Brown, Simmons, & Methvin, 1979), other more advanced skills that are likely to be delayed for these children are:

- jumping skills
- kicking a stationary ball
- walking on tiptoe
- cutting with scissors

Whenever norm-referenced tests standardized on sighted children are used with children who are visually impaired or blind, results will need to be interpreted in light of the fact that certain motor skills often require more time to develop for these children. The comparison with the norms for sighted children must be made only with qualifications, because the experiences for developing motor skills are so different for visually impaired and blind children.

Adaptive Behavior

Adaptive behavior as used in this text includes both self-help skills and social behavior.

Adaptive Behaviors Often Delayed.   In terms of self-help skills, there are several that may require more time for some children to learn because of visual impairment or blindness:

- Often these children have difficulty learning to chew solid foods. Factors that contribute to the delay in learning to chew are the lack of visual enticement from the food and the inability to see others chewing their food.
- Learning to handle a spoon may take longer than it does for sighted children. Scooping can be particularly difficult.
- Picking up and replacing a cup on the table may also take longer to learn (Brown, et al., 1979). Children with a visual impairment or who are blind tend to throw a cup more frequently.
- Ashman (1982) notes that a delay in the development of fine motor skills can result in a delay in the acquisition of self-help skills that require fine-motor ability.
- Brown et al. (1979) note that reaching for a familiar person and initiation of interaction with an adult by offering a toy may take longer to develop.

When assessing self-help skills, it is important to note the degree to which the parents encourage and prompt the child to learn these skills. Bauman (1973) has pointed out that in trying to be helpful to visually handicapped children, adults may interfere with, and even prevent, the usual learning experiences. Hence, parents who are overly helpful will need assistance themselves in allowing the child to develop self-help skills to avoid unnecessary delay in the child's development.

In terms of social skills, it is helpful to consider the child's use of gestures and facial expressions. Without the use of these behaviors, a child may appear unusual, and it could cause difficulty in communication with peers. Many gestures must be taught to children with little or no vision because they will not have visual models to follow. Some facial expressions will appear even without visual models, but some may not.

Play Skills

Children learn to interact with the environment through play. Piaget (1952) has described the importance of play to cognitive development. Play has an important role in the development of language as well.

Without visual stimulation, a child with little or no vision is unlikely to interact with the environment as would a sighted child. In the extreme case, if a child with little or no vision is not encouraged to explore the environment and to play, this will result in a passive child who is not curious about his or her surroundings. If this child fails to actively explore the environment, then motor, language, cognitive, and social skills will be impaired. Hence, it is particularly important to assess the play behavior of a child with a serious visual problem.

In assessing play behavior it must be kept in mind that a delay in the development of fine motor skills will delay the development of play skills that require fine motor behaviors (Ashman, 1982).

The use of toys during testing that provide auditory stimulation and that are relatively large (e.g., Giant Texture Beads and large peg boards available from the American Printing House for the Blind) will aid a child in locating and using them. As noted earlier, some children with little or no vision usually do not like furry toys (Scott et al., 1985), but toys that provide other types of tactile input are helpful (e.g., Textured Pegs and Large Textured Blocks also available from the American Printing House for the Blind). Figure 5 displays the Textured Pegs.

Because of the visual handicap, it is unlikely that these children will search for toys that are out of reach (Scott et al., 1985; Brown et al., 1979). When a toy moves or is moved out of reach of the child, it is as if the toy no longer exists. Thus, if a child does not search for toys, this is a skill that must be taught.

Thorough exploration of toys is also important for tactile and kinesthetic input. It may be necessary to prompt some children to turn objects around and to explore them using their tactile sense.

There are a number of criterion-referenced tests and informal measures that can be used to assess play skills. Because there are so many play behaviors, it may be necessary to use several measures in order to comprehensively assess this area.

Language Development

Though the language development of children with little or no vision is very similar to that of sighted children, there are some differences, particularly in the rate of development.

Figure 5. Textured pegs. (Courtesy the American Printing House for the Blind.)

Scott et al. (1985) note that these children learn to recognize their names at about 12 months of age; sighted children typically acquire this skill between 7 and 9 months of age. Though these children babble at about the same age as sighted children, some children with little or no vision may be delayed in speaking their first words and a delay in labeling objects may also be noted (Fewell, 1983).

Scott et al. (1985) suggest that children with visual impairments or blindness should learn position concepts early. Thus, assessment of a young child's knowledge of these concepts is helpful. It may take a visually impaired or blind child longer to learn concepts such as *left, right,* and *up,* so there is a need to begin teaching them as early as possible. Further, these children must rely heavily on these concepts, more so than sighted children, to function effectively.

The use of personal pronouns such as *I* and *you* may also take longer to develop (Fewell, 1983; Goldman & Duda, 1978).

Though blind children use color words, Anderson and Olson (1981) found that they made fewer references to color in describing objects.

Norm-Referenced Tests

Table 3 shows areas assessed by various norm-referenced tests. Those tests selected were (a) designed to be individually administered (to meet the

TABLE 3
Norm-Referenced Tests for Infants and Preschoolers

	Areas Assessed			
Tests	Cognitive	Motor	Adaptive	Language
Basic School Skills Inventory–D (4 to 6 years, 11 months)			X	X
Battelle Developmental Inventory (birth through 8 years)	X	X	X	X
Bayley Scales of Infant Development (2 to 30 months)	X	X		
Carrow Elicited Language Inventory (3 to 7 years, 11 months)				X
Cognitive Abilities Relevant to Education (2 and 3 years)	X			
Stanford-Binet Intelligence Scale (2 years to superior adult)	X			
Test of Language Development– Primary (4 to 8 years, 11 months)				X
Vineland Social Maturity Scale (3 to 18 years, 11 months)		X	X	X
Weschler Preschool and Primary Scale of Intelligence–Verbal Scale (4 to 6½ years)	X			

legal requirements for special education placement), (b) published within the last 15 years (so that the content and norms were reasonably current, i.e., not out-of-date), and (c) able to circumvent a visual handicap (to ensure that a visually impaired or blind child would be capable of making the required responses). If a test required vision on some items, but included a relatively large number of visually impaired and blind children in the sample, it was included (e.g., the *Vineland Social Maturity Scale*, Sparrow, Balla, & Cicchetti, 1984). Some tests that are frequently mentioned in the literature (e.g., *A Social Maturity Scale for Blind Preschool Children*, Maxfield & Bucholz, 1957; and the *Interim Hayes-Binet*, Hayes, 1942) are 25 years old or older and therefore out-of-date. Such tests are pre-Sputnik and unlikely to be applicable today. Two tests were exceptions to these criteria: the *Bayley Scales of Infant Development* (Bayley, 1969) and the *Wechsler Preschool and Primary Scale of Intelligence*–Verbal Scale (Wechsler, 1967). Although they are more than 15 years old and the Bayley has items that require vision, these tests were included because the test options for assessing cognitive development are so limited that these tests must be given consideration.

Many children with visual impairments can be tested with instruments designed for sighted children. In some cases magnification or enlargement of test materials, special lighting, and other special procedures may be required.

The following norm-referenced tests were reviewed in detail using the criteria presented in Chapter 1 to evaluate technical adequacy of tests. Adaptation of items on tests that were not designed for infants and children with little or no vision are included in the reviews. Descriptions of administration procedures, responses required, materials used, and scoring procedures are presented.

Basic School Skills Inventory–Diagnostic

Authors: Donald D. Hammill and James E. Leigh

Publisher: PRO-ED
            5341 Industrial Oaks Blvd.
            Austin, TX 78735

Copyright: 1983

General Description. The *Basic School Skills Inventory–Diagnostic* (BSSI–D) was planned for children between the ages of 4–0 to 6–11. This test is made up of six subtests: Daily Living Skills, Spoken Language, Reading, Writing, Mathematics, and Classroom Behavior. Three of these subtests do not require vision (or require minor modification for children with little or no vision): Daily Living Skills, Spoken Language, and Classroom Behavior. Hence, only these three subtests will be reviewed. The test is designed to be scored by someone who has observed the student in the classroom over a period of time, such as the classroom teacher.

Scores from the BSSI–D can be interpreted as percentiles, standard scores (mean = 10, standard deviation = 3) for subtests, and as a quotient for the total score.

If the entire inventory were used, the administration time would be about 30 minutes. About half this time would be needed for the three subtests that do not require vision. Many items can be scored based on prior knowledge of the student and from observation in the classroom.

Materials needed for the three subtests are: the manual, a recording form, primary scissors, paper, a pencil, a penny, a nickel, a dime, a braille clock or watch (or one with raised numbers), and a picture made of raised lines.

Description of Subtests

Daily Living Skills. This 20-item subtest assesses a child's ability to participate in daily classroom activities. The manual suggests that "Children who do well on these items are likely to be those who are considered independent and responsible" (p. 21). Examples include "Does the child wash hands and face properly?" and "Does the child use a handkerchief or tissue properly?" Three items would be problematic for children with little or no vision unless adaptations were made. "Is the child able to fold paper and cut with scissors?" should not be a problem for folding paper, though it may be difficult to make an exact fold and this should be considered in scoring. Cutting with scissors could be adapted by drawing the square to be cut with a black crayon, making a heavy line that could be felt with the fingers for a visually impaired child. A raised line square would be needed for a blind child. "Can the child follow directions to underline, draw a circle and draw an X?" are not relevant skills for a blind child. Underlining in braille is done by use of an italic sign before a word. Ability to follow directions should be tested using different tasks. The third troublesome item is "Can the child tell time by looking at a clock?" This would require use of a braille clock or watch or one with raised numbers.

Spoken Language. There are 20 items on this subtest that assess the type of spoken language used by the child in the classroom. Examples include "Can the child artiulate speech sounds correctly?" and "Can the child use possessive forms correctly?" Two items need special consideration for children with little or no vision. "Does the child use the pronoun *I* correctly?" is a skill that is apt to be delayed for these children. This must be considered in interpreting results. "Can the child describe the contents of a picture?" would be impossible for a child without vision unless the picture were adapted. A simple raised line drawing could be used instead.

Classroom Behavior. All 20 items on this subtest could be used for children with little or no vision without modification of the items. Examples of items include "Can the child wait his turn?" and "Does the child follow classroom rules?" Some items need to be scored in light of the fact that the child has a visual problem. For example, "Can the child go through the normal school day without becoming overly tired and listless?" may be particularly difficult for a visually impaired child because extended use of usable vision can be very tiring. This is an important issue to consider in planning the child's classroom program, but a visually impaired child should not be penalized for this physical limitation in scoring the item.

Technical Adequacy

Standardization. The 376 children were selected to correspond to data in the 1980 *Statistical Abstract of the United States.* The demographic characteristics of the sample approximate these data for sex and urban-rural residence. For occupation of parents, there were too few white-collar parents (28% instead of 51%) and too many blue collar parents (61% compared to 36%). For race, black students were slightly under represented (6% compared to 12%). In terms of geographic distribution, the South was overrepresented (53% compared to 33%), and the West underrepresented (1% compared to 19%).

Reliability. No test-retest data are provided. Internal consistency correlation ranges were as follows: Daily Living Skills, .85 to .90; Spoken Language, .81 to .93; and Classroom Behavior, .93 to .97.

Standard errors of measurement are provided for all subtests by age level.

Validity. Content validity seems to be good because teacher input was used to develop the items, and the items were field tested four times to eliminate those items teachers thought were vague or unimportant. Further, the items were found to be adequate in terms of discriminating power and difficulty according to an item analysis.

For criterion-related validity, teacher rankings were correlated with BSSI–D results. Correlations were .35 for Daily Living Skills, .38 for Spoken Language, and .37 for Classroom Behavior.

In terms of construct validity, the scores were found to increase with age, and correlations for interrelationship of the subtests ranged from .34 to .83. The BSSI–D was found to discriminate between a group of 12 Learning Disabled and 12 "normal" students for all subtests except Classroom Behavior.

Conclusions. The BSSI–D could provide some useful information regarding the child's behavior and language skills in a classroom setting (i.e., preschool, kindergarten, or first grade). Because information is obtained from the teacher or someone who has observed the child for some time in the classroom, it is particularly relevant. However, the scores obtained would need to be combined with information from other tests because of limitations in the standardization sample and reliability data. More information with larger samples is needed on diagnostic and criterion-related validity. Besides the scores, the BSSI–D would provide some information for planning classroom activities. Some special considerations were noted that are important when scoring the subtests for children who have little or no vision.

Battelle Developmental Inventory

Authors: Jean Newborg, John R. Stock, Linda Wnek,
          John Guidubaldi, and John Svinicki

Publisher: DLM Teaching Resources
           One DLM Park
           Allen, TX 75002

Copyright: 1984

General Description. The *Battelle Developmental Inventory* (BDI) is an individually-administered test battery for children from birth through 8 years of age. The purposes of the inventory are to provide data to aid in making decisions regarding special education eligibility and placement, and to plan specific classroom programs for children.

The inventory consists of five domains: Cognitive, Communication, Motor, Adaptive, and Personal-Social. Each domain can be divided into several subdomains. Information for scoring can be obtained by directly testing a child, through interviews, and through observation in the natural setting. It is suggested in the manual that "examiners should use the procedures that will yield the best data" (p. 8). Scores are given for the total test, each domain, and each subdomain. Scores are in the form of percentiles, standard scores (Z, t, deviation quotients, and normal curve equivalents), and age equivalents. The BDI also has a Screening Test.

The Screening Test takes from 10 to 30 minutes to administer. The BDI requires 1 hour or less for children under 3 and over 5 years of age. For children between 3 and 5, 1½ to 2 hours are needed.

Each item is scored either 2 (full credit), 1 (attempted or an emerging skill), or 0 (fail). This is a useful scoring system for planning classroom activities because items scored as emerging would be appropriate to concentrate on first for remediation.

Materials for the BDI include a manual, six test books, and an envelope of visual materials. Toys and other materials needed are those "commonly found in preschool and primary level programs" (p. 2) and must be obtained by the examiner. Supplementary materials for visually impaired and blind children must also be obtained by the examiner. Lists of these materials are presented in the manual. An examiner would have to plan to prepare the materials well in advance of testing because of the time needed to make or obtain them. For example, on the Cognitive Domain two items require braille cards, one a raised figure, and one a braille clock. On the Motor Domain 10 raised figures are needed, and a beeper ball is required for several items.

Both general adaptation procedures and specific adaptations for certain items are suggested for handicapped children. The purpose of the adaptations is "to provide a means by which specific barriers to assessing a given behavior, posed by given handicapping conditions, can be overcome without changing the behavior that is being assessed" (p. 15). Unfortunately, this is not the case for severely visually impaired or blind children. For these children, each domain contains items for certain age levels that must be scored 0 because of the child's handicap. Some of these items are scored 0 because the adaptation indicates that it is "for instructional use only," while other items have no adaptations and require vision. Most of these items appear in the Cognitive Domain, making it almost impossible to obtain a valid score for any age level for this type of child. If no Cognitive score is obtained, a Total score cannot be obtained either. If enough of these items were scored 0 and a test score determined, it would be an underestimate of the child's ability. In the other domains there are from one to four of these items. Hence, valid scores might be obtained on this test for visually impaired children with good usable vision, but not for children with no useful vision. However, the BDI could still provide useful information for children with little or no vision for the purpose of program planning, or for describing a range of performance based on the age levels of items passed.

Descriptions of Screening and Domain Tests

Screening Test. The 96-item Screening Test contains two items per age level from each of the five domains. Its use is to aid in determining whether to give the entire BDI. If a child scores one standard deviation or more below the mean, this suggests that the entire BDI be given. Because of the limited number of items per age level, the Screening Test will not be of much use, especially for a child with little or no vision. It would be risky to make a decision on the child's abilities based on such a small sample of behavior. A better approach would be to leave out the Screening Test and go directly to the BDI domains.

Cognitive Domain. This domain taps abilities "conceptual in nature" (p. 6) and consists of four subdomains: Perceptual Discrimination (e.g., feeling and exploring objects, matching words), Memory (e.g., following an auditory stimulus, repeating digits), Reasoning & Academic Skills (e.g., uncovering a hidden toy, simple math problems), Conceptual Development (e.g., identifying objects by use, sorting by shape and color). There are 56 items in the domain, but the number of items per age level varies from 3 to 12, with the majority of levels having fewer than 7 items. Thus, the number of items provides a very limited sample of a child's skills, especially if the child has no useful vision. Following is a list of the number of items that must be scored 0 for a child with no useful vision:

Age level (months)	Number of items scored 0
0–5	2 of 6
6–11	0 of 3
12–23	0 of 3
24–35	3 of 5
36–47	0 of 4
48–59	0 of 8
60–71	1 of 12
72–83	3 of 8
84–95	1 of 7

Depending on the child's age, it is likely that if a score were determined from this domain for a child with little or no vision it would be an underestimate of the child's ability. Scores for the four subdomains within the Cognitive Domain would be based on so few items that they would be meaningless. Even scores for children with at least some useful vision would have to be interpreted with great caution because of the limited number of items involved. The number of items administered is further limited by the basal and ceiling rules.

Communication. This domain assesses both the receptive and expressive aspects of language and is made up of 59 items. The Receptive subdomain taps discrimination (e.g., discriminates nonsense and real words) and meaning (e.g., follows two-part commands). The Expressive subdomain taps sounds (e.g., produces one or more vowel sounds), grammar-rules (e.g., uses plural ending with *s* or *z* sound), and meaning-usage (e.g., uses 10 or more words). The number of items per age level ranges from 4 to 10, with the majority having fewer than 7 items. Only 3 items in this domain would be scored 0 because of lack of vision: 1 of 7 items at the 4- to 5-year level, and 2 of 10 items at the 5- to 6-year level. Considering the basal and ceiling rules and the limited number of items, scores from this domain are also questionable.

Motor. This domain assesses use of large and small muscles and is made up of five subdomains: Muscle Control (e.g., holds head up for at least 5 seconds when on stomach), Body Coordination (e.g., turns a somersault), Locomotion (e.g., runs a distance of 10 feet without falling), Fine Muscle (e.g., folds a sheet of paper), and Perceptual Motor (e.g., reaches for and touches an object). The domain consists of 82 items, with a range of 6 to 11 items per age level. The majority of levels have more than 7 items. Thus, the domain score will sample quite a few behaviors, even with the basals and ceilings applied. Whether the subdomains sampled enough behaviors to yield a score that can be interpreted will have to be examined for each child tested. Only 3 items must be scored 0 if a child has little or no vision: 1 of 9 items at the 5- to 6-year level, 1 of 7 at the 6- to 7-year level, and 1 of 6 at the 7- to 8-year level.

Adaptive. Five subdomains make up the 59 item Adaptive Domain. Subdomains are: Attention (e.g., visually attends to an object for 5 seconds or more), Eating (e.g., anticipates feeding), Dressing (e.g., puts on shoes without assistance), Personal Responsibility (e.g., demonstrates caution and avoids common dangers), and Toileting (e.g., sleeps through the night without wetting the bed). The number of items per age level ranges from 3 to 10, with the majority having fewer than 7 items. Again, with the basal and ceiling rules, the small number of items per age level, and the five subdomains, the subdomain scores will probably be based on too few items to be valid measures. Further, at the 0- to 5-month level 2 of the 5 items are scored 0 if the child has no usable vision and 2 of 7 items are scored 0 at the 6- to 11-month level.

Personal-Social. This 85-item domain taps abilities related to "meaningful social interactions" (p. 5). There are six subdomains: Adult Interaction (e.g., explores adult facial features), Expression of Feelings/Affect (e.g., enjoys playing with other children), Self-Concept (e.g., identifies self in mirror), Peer Interaction (e.g., shares property with others), Coping (e.g., complies with adult directives), and Social Role (e.g., dramatizes in play). The number of items per age level ranges from 4 to 15, with the majority having more than 7 items. Depending on a child's age, the domain score might sample a sufficient number of behaviors, but the subdomains probably will not. Only 1 item on this domain receives a 0 if a child has no vision, and this is at the 6 to 11 month level. The content of this subtest taps important skills that are often not systematically considered in an assessment. Personal-social skills are especially important for visually impaired and blind students. Thus, this domain seems worthwhile to administer.

Technical Adequacy

Standardization. Data were collected from December of 1982 until March of 1983. The sample corresponds closely to the 1981 U.S. census data in terms of geographical distribution, sex, and race (8.9% black, 6.4% Spanish origin, and .7% other). About 75% were urban and 25% rural. No data are presented on socioeconomic status except that the manual states that test sites were selected that had a wide range of socioeconomic levels. The number of subjects per age level for 24 months through 95 months approximates 100 (range 90–102). For birth to 23 months there are only 49 to 54 subjects per level. Either more subjects should have been used or some age levels collapsed in preparing the norm tables. Thus, the sample appears to be representative in terms of geographical distribution, sex, urban/rural, and race. Data are needed on socioeconomic status, and more subjects are needed for age levels below 24 months.

Reliability. Test-retest data are given by age level for 183 children (about 18 per age level) with a four week interval. Correlation ranges for the domains were: Cognitive .84–.98, Communication .76–.96, Motor .88–.99, Adaptive .84–.99, and Personal-Social .92–.99. Range for the BDI total was .90 to .99. Data are provided for subdomains also.

Interrater reliability is presented by age level for subdomains, domains, and totals. The range for the total score was .93–.99. Domains ranges were: Cognitive .86–1.0, Communication .85–.98, Motor .91–.99, Adaptive .93–.99, and Personal-Social .86–.99.

Standard errors of measurement are given by age level for subdomains, domains, and total test.

Validity. Items were selected based on review of existing tests and then evaluated by numerous experts in each area. The instrument was pilot tested several times, the last time with 500 children from birth to 8 years of age. Item difficulty and item-total score correlations were used for assigning age levels and sequencing the items. These procedures would suggest good content validity. The test does seem to sample a range of important behaviors. The problem is that there are too few items per age level to adequately sample the skills.

In terms of construct validity, factor analysis indicates that the subdomains intercorrelate quite well. The domains tend to be more accurate for children over 2 years of age. The intercorrelation of BDI component scores is quite high. Age comparisons suggest that scores tend to increase with age.

In terms of diagnostic validity, a study was carried out with clinical (160 children with a variety of handicaps) and nonclinical samples. All domain and total scores indicated significant differences between the two groups. For criterion-related validity, comparisons were made with the *Vineland Social Maturity Scale* (1965 version) ($n = 37$), the *Developmental Activities Screening Inventory* (DASI) ($n = 36$), the *Stanford-Binet Intelligence Scale* ($n = 23$), the *Wechsler Intelligence Scale for Children–Revised* ($n = 10$ for Verbal and Performance, 13 Full Scale), and the *Peabody Picture Vocabulary Test* (1981 version) ($n = 15$). The BDI correlated most highly with the *Vineland* and the DASI. This was true even for the Cognitive Domain. Although acceptable correlations were obtained with the *Binet*, WISC–R, and PPVT (though all of these studies used only a small number of subjects), the BDI seems to be measuring skills that are more similar to tests tapping adaptive behaviors and motor skills than to intelligence tests.

Conclusions. Standardization of the BDI appears representative except that no socioeconomic data are available on the sample and an insufficient number of children below 24 months of age were involved. Reliability data are excellent. Additional validity information is needed on the test's ability to discriminate between specific diagnostic groups, predictive ability, and criterion-related validity with larger samples. Because of the small number of items most subdomain and some domain scores would be meaningless.

This inventory has the advantage of describing how many of the items can be adapted for children with little or no vision, though not all items can be adapted. Valid scores could be obtained for many visually impaired children. The age-referenced items could be used to help describe a range of performance for children with little or no vision. Some information could be obtained for both groups for program planning, but criterion-referenced information would also be needed.

Bayley Scales of Infant Development

Author: Nancy Bayley

Publisher: The Psychological Corporation
555 Academic Court
San Antonio, TX 78204

Copyright: 1969

General Description. The *Bayley Scales of Infant Development* are individually administered and designed for children from 2 to 30 months of age. Normal or above average children of 24 months of age or older may not achieve a ceiling on this test. The purpose of the *Scales* is to provide norm-referenced scores to describe a child's current level of performance in terms of mental and motor development. The *Scales* consist of three parts: the Mental Scale, the Motor Scale, and the Infant Behavior Record. The Infant Behavior Record is an informal measure rather than a standardized test, thus it is critiqued under Criterion-Referenced Tests and Informal Measures later in the book.

Scores for the Mental and Motor scales are standard scores in the form of deviation quotients with a mean of 100 and a standard deviation of 16. Each item is scored *pass, fail,* or *other. Other* includes omissions, refusals, and parent report. Only *pass* items are considered in scoring.

Administration time for both scales is from 45 to 75 minutes. Tests are to be given with the mother, or a mother substitute, present.

Materials include a test manual, record books for each of the three sections, and numerous toys contained in the kit. Also needed for testing, but not included in the kit, are sheets of 8½ x 11" paper and some facial tissues for the Mental Scale, and a set of stairs and a walking board for the Motor Scale. Examiners must exercise caution when using some of the test materials to ensure the child's safety. The rattle that usually comes with the kit is one considered dangerous by the Consumer Product Safety Commission because it is small enough that it could become lodged in a child's throat. The cubes, beads, and doll head (for "Mending broken doll") are also small enough to fit in a child's mouth and could cause a child to choke.

No adaptations are given in the manual for using the *Bayley Scales* with visually impaired or blind children. A large number of the items require vision.

Description of the Scales

Mental Scale. The Mental Scale consists of 163 items. A wide variety of skills are tapped, but it is primarily sensory and motor abilities that are emphasized. It is suggested in the manual that the following skills are tested: sensory perceptual, object constancy, memory, learning, problem solving, vocalizations, early verbal communication, forming generalizations, and classification. There are too few items in each of the areas tested to be able to draw conclusions for planning specific educational programs. The results can be used only to describe a child's current overall level of performance.

Caution is needed in interpreting results from this scale because it is questionable whether some of the items are measuring mental abilities related to later intelligence (e.g., reaches for a second cube, places pegs in 30 rather than 40 seconds, drops 6 beads in a box). This may be one factor that accounts for the poor predictive validity of the Bayley Mental Scale. Fagan (1982) points out that studies correlating the *Bayley* (given during the first year) and the *Binet* (given about three years of age) show average correlations of about .18 for high-risk and clinic samples. He suggests that these sensory and motor skills shown later in life may be unrelated to intelligence.

Motor Scale. Of the 81 items on this scale, only 14 require vision.

Technical Aspects

Standardization. A total of 1,262 subjects participated, with from 83 to 95 children per age level. Thus, there were not quite a sufficient number of subjects for each age level used. Subjects were selected to correspond to the 1960 census data in terms of sex, race, educational attainment of the head of the household, and urban-rural residence. Children in rural areas were not adequately represented. Subjects were not selected based on geographic location, so some obvious problems exist. Below is a chart comparing the sample to both the 1960 and 1983 census data:

	Bayley Percentage	1960 Percentage	1983 Percentage
Northeast	28	23	22
Northcentral	18	30	27
South	17	32	33
West	37	16	19

It can be seen that a nationally representative sample was not obtained because there were only about two-thirds the number needed from the Northcentral region, half the number necessary from the South, and twice as many children as there should have been from the West.

Reliability. No test-retest data are reported in the manual on the current version of the test. On an earlier version of the *Bayley*, a one-week retest was done for 28 8-month-old babies. Agreement obtained was 76% on the Mental Scale and 75% on the Motor Scale. The one-week interval is too short and the reliabilities are insufficient for making eligibility decisions for special education. Furthermore, data are needed for each age level, not just for 8 months of age.

Interrater reliability for 90 8-month-olds was calculated using percent agreement. Results for the Mental Scale were 89% agreement and 93% agreement for the Motor Scale.

Standard errors of measurement are provided for both the Mental and Motor scales by age level.

Split-half reliabilities range from .81 to .93 for the Mental Scale and from .68 to .92 for the Motor Scale.

Validity. Predictive and content validity issues were discussed under the description of the Mental Scale.

One concurrent validity study is cited in the manual for the Mental scale with the *Stanford-Binet* for 120 children. Correlations ranged from .47 to .64.

Conclusions.   Given the problems with the standardization, reliability, and validity, and because of the lack of adaptations for children with little or no vision on the Mental Scale, the *Bayley* is not a useful test for children who have visual problems. Presently there are so few options for assessing cognitive development for infants and preschoolers that some information from the test will probably have to be used in the assessment of visually impaired and blind infants. However, the information must be evaluated in light of the limitations of the test and in conjunction with information from testing other areas of development with othe measures. No valid score will be possible for children with little or no vision on the Mental Scale, though it may be possible to obtain a valid score for many visually impaired children. Because the items are age-referenced, the age levels of items on which a child with little or no vision was successful could be used to describe a range of performance for the child. Most items on the Motor Scale could be used with visually impaired and blind children.

Carrow Elicited Language Inventory

Author: Elizabeth Carrow

Publisher: DLM/Teaching Resources
            P.O. Box 4000
            One DLM Park
            Allen, TX 75002

Copyright: 1974

General Description. The *Carrow Elicited Language Inventory* (CELI) was written for children between the ages of 3 and 7-11. Its purpose is to assess a child's ability to use correct grammar in speech. No vision is required to take the test.

The test consists of 52 items, each of which is verbally presented by the examiner. The child's task is to repeat the material. Though various areas of language are assessed, the CELI is not broken into subtests.

Results can be reported in terms of percentiles or stanines. Mean scores are provided for each age level for comparison purposes.

Administration time is about 30 to 45 minutes. The child's responses should be recorded on an audiotape.

Materials needed are the manual, a record book, a scoring/analysis form, an audiotape, and tape recorder.

Description of Items. Fifty-one of the items are sentences and one is a phrase. The word length of items varies from 2 to 10 words. The grammatical forms tested by CELI are: pronouns, prepositions, conjunctions, articles, adverbs, WH-questions, negatives, nouns, adjectives and predicate adjectives, verbs, infinitives, and a gerund. The test was planned to aid in designing individual classroom programs as well as to provide a norm-referenced score. Use of the results for planning programs is limited by the fact that the number of items per skill varies from 1 to 50. Hence, for those skills that are tested with a sufficient number of items, CELI results would be useful. However, almost half of the skills are tested less than five times. For the major categories listed above there appear to be a sufficient number of items; for the subcategories there is not likely to be a sufficient sample of the behaviors.

Technical Adequacy

Standardization. The CELI does not have a representative national sample. All 475 children in the sample were white, from middle-socioeconomic homes where standard American English was the only language, and from Houston, Texas. No data are provided on the sex of the sample.

Reliability. Test-retest data were obtained with a two-week retest interval. A correlation was obtained of .98 for 5 children at each age level for ages 3, 4, 5, 6, and 7.

Interrater correlations of .98 (n = 10) and .99 (n = 20) were obtained in two studies.

Validity. Scores tend to increase with age.

One study is reported that showed that CELI is able to discriminate between a group of children with normal language and a group of children considered to be language disordered.

In terms of concurrent validity, results of rank ordering by clinical judgment and results of the CELI correlated .77. A correlation of .79 was obtained between CELI and results of the *Developmental Sentence Scoring Test.*

Conclusions. CELI could provide an estimate of the level of grammar a child uses in speech. The standardization is not at all representative of the children in the U.S. and is appropriate for only white, English speaking children. Dialect differences would affect performance. Reliability and validity data are encouraging. Results would suggest areas of strength and difficulty with regard to use of grammatical forms (e.g., pronouns and WH-questions). Specific words within those areas that are troublesome would have to be determined from further informal testing.

Test of Language Development–Primary

Authors: Phyllis L. Newcomer and Donald D. Hammill

Publisher: PRO-ED
         5341 Industrial Oaks Blvd.
         Austin, TX 78735

Copyright: 1977, 1982

General Description. The *Test of Language Development–Primary* (TOLD–P) is appropriate for use with children between the ages of 4 and

8-11. The purpose of this norm-referenced test is to comprehensively assess language.

The TOLD–P is made up of seven subtests. Four of the subtests do not require vision and it is these subtests that will be reviewed. These subtests include: Oral Vocabulary, Sentence Imitation, Grammatic Completion, and Word Discrimination.

Results can be reported as language ages, percentiles, and standard scores (mean = 10, standard deviation = 3) for the subtests. Results of subtests can be combined to form composites, and results for composites and the total are reported in terms of quotients. It is possible to obtain a Speaking Quotient using subtests that do not require vision.

Materials needed for subtests that do not require vision are a manual and recording form.

Description of Subtests. Though the type of presentation of items and the response required may be appropriate on the following subtests, the content of particular items may be a problem for some visually impaired and blind students. For example, *castle* and *village* on the Oral Vocabulary subtest may be particularly difficult for a child with a severe visual loss. Hence, caution must be used in interpreting results.

Oral Vocabulary. This 20-item subtest assesses a child's ability to use correct semantics in speech. The examiner says a word such as *sugar* and the child is asked to tell what it means.

Sentence Imitation. There are 30 items on this subtest that assess a child's ability to use correct syntax in speech. The examiner verbally presents a sentence and the child must repeat it exactly. The manual states that the assumption is ". . . that it is easier for children to repeat or imitate grammatic forms that are part of their linguistic repertoires than it is to repeat those that are unfamiliar" (p. 4).

Grammatic Completion. Thirty items tap a child's ability to use correct grammar in speech. The examiner reads a sentence with a word missing and the child is to complete the sentence. An example is; "A girl plays the piano every day. Yesterday she _____ ."

Word Discrimination. For this 20-item subtest the examiner reads a word pair such as "falls-false" and the student is to indicate whether the words are the same or different. These items assess a child's ability to hear differences in phonemes. This subtest is not appropriate for children older than 6 years of age.

Technical Adequacy

Standardization. There were 1,836 children who participated in the standardization. The sample closely approximates the data in the 1980 *Statis-*

tical Abstracts of the United States on the following demographic characteristics: sex, urban-rural residence, race, geographic distribution, and occupation of parents.

Reliability. Test-retest data were collected on 21 children from 4 to 8 years old with a 5-day retest interval. Correlation coefficients for the subtests that do not require vision were: Oral Vocabulary .93, Sentence Imitation .98, Grammatic Completion .96, and Word Discrimination .94. Although these data are certainly encouraging, test-retest data are needed by age level with about a 2-week interval.

Internal consistency coefficients for these particular subtests ranged from .67 to .96. Speaking Composite correlations ranged from .85 to .95.

Standard errors of measurement are provided for subtests and composites by age level.

Validity. Items were analyzed in terms of item difficulty and discriminating power and found to be acceptable. Further, an extensive rationale is given for the development of the items based on a review of the literature and data from several field tests. Fifty professionals in the field of language critiqued the items and found them to be consistent with the model used to construct the TOLD–P.

For criterion-related validity, the TOLD–P was compared to several other tests that tapped similar areas. For the subtests that do not require vision, the following correlation ranges were obtained: Oral Vocabulary and WISC–Vocabulary, .67 to .79; Sentence Imitation (SI) and *Northwestern Syntax Screening Test*–Expressive, .55 to .77; SI and *Detroit Tests of Learning Aptitude*–Related Syllables, .68 to .84; Grammatic Completion and *Illinois Test of Psycholinguistic Ability*–Grammatic Closure, .49 to .78; and Word Discrimination and *Auditory Discrimination Test*, .57 to .70.

In terms of construct validity, the mean scores increase with age. The intercorrelation of the subtests ranged from .45 to .55. Because language is related to intelligence and achievement, TOLD–P results were correlated with scores from the WISC and various achievement tests. WISC correlations ranged from .29 to .82. TOLD–P correlations with various achievement tests ranged from .42 to .68. Various studies are cited in the manual to demonstrate that the test discriminates groups of children with different language problems. Two factor analytic studies reported in the manual tend to support the structure of the TOLD–P.

Conclusions. The standardization and validity data on the TOLD–P are very good. More test-retest data are needed. This well-thought-out test could provide very useful information on areas of strength and difficulty for language of visually impaired and blind children. The four subtests described do not require vision. However, the content of failed items should be carefully considered to ensure that the items were appropriate for a child with a severe visual loss.

Vineland Social Maturity Scale

Because this instrument is designed primarily for students above 4 years of age, the critique for the *Vineland Scale* appears in Chapter 5.

Wechsler Preschool and Primary Scale of Intelligence

Author: David Wechsler

Publisher: The Psychological Corporation
            555 Academic Court
            San Antonio, TX 78204

Copyright: 1963, 1967

General Description. This individually-administered test is designed for children from 4 to 6½ years of age. This is an extension of the *Wechsler Intelligence Scale for Children*. It is made up of 11 subtests, 6 of which make up the Verbal Scale and 5 the Performance Scale. Only the Verbal Scale will be reviewed because the Performance Scale requires vision and could not be used to circumvent a visual problem. Subtests for the Verbal Scale are: Information, Vocabulary, Arithmetic, Similarities, Comprehension, and Sentences (a supplementary subtest). Sentences can be used as an additional subtest, but is not used in calculating an IQ score.

Results are in terms of scaled scores or intelligence quotients. Scores can be obtained for each subtest, for the Verbal and Performance Scales, and for the Full Scale Score.

Administration time is approximately 50 to 75 minutes. Use of only the Verbal Scale would require approximately half this amount of time.

The materials for the Verbal Scale include the manual, record forms, and a set of blocks. No adaptations are presented for visually impaired or blind children. However, if the Verbal Scale is used with a child with little or no vision, four special cards with raised drawings will be needed for the first four items on the Arithmetic Subtest.

Description of Subtests

Information. There are 23 items on this subtest where the child is asked questions such as "How many ears do you have?" The first item requires the child to touch his or her nose. Other than this item, only verbal responses are needed.

Vocabulary. This subtest consists of 22 items for which the child is asked to tell the examiner what words mean. Examples include "shoe," "donkey," and "nuisance." Responses are scored 2, 1, or 0 depending on the content of the answer.

Arithmetic. There are 20 items, 12 of which require a verbal response. Four items with pictures (raised figures needed for children with little or no vision) require the child to point. On three other items the child is asked to count a certain number of blocks and for one item to give the examiner some blocks.

Similarities. There are 16 items on this subtest. The format for the first 10 items requires that the child complete a sentence such as, "Milk and water are both good to _____." For the remaining six items the child must indicate how two things are alike (e.g., piano-violin). These are scored 2, 1, or 0 based on the quality of the response.

Comprehension. For the 15 items on this subtest, children must answer questions given verbally by the examiner. An example is, "Why should children who are sick stay home?" Answers are scored 2, 1, or 0.

Sentences. This supplementary test was designed in place of Digit Span on the WISC. There are ten sentences that are given verbally by the examiner and the child is asked to repeat them. This subtest provides an estimate of a child's verbal memory. This is useful information to consider in program planning for visually impaired or blind children who must rely on auditory input for learning.

Technical Adequacy

Standardization. The sample for the WPPSI contained 100 boys and 100 girls per age level, for a total of 1,200 children. The demographic data correspond very closely to the 1960 census data in terms of geographic distribution, father's education, and urban/rural residence. Further, there is a close correspondence for race (white and nonwhite) by geographic distribution and by urban/rural residence. The sample seems to be a good representation of the U.S. population for these age levels.

Reliability. Test-retest data are given for only 50 children between 5½ and 5¾ years of age. The retest interval was 48 to 117 days. Correlations for the Verbal subtests ranged from .60 to .89. The correlation for the Verbal IQ was .86. More data are needed by age level.

    Internal consistency data on Verbal subtests ranged from .77 to .88. Verbal IQ correlations ranged from .93 to .95.

Standard errors of measurement are given for each subtest and the Verbal scale. These data are presented by age level.

Validity. The average intercorrelation of the subtests on the Verbal Scale ranged from .46 to .60. Average intercorrelations of the Verbal IQ and the Verbal subtests ranged from .62 to .73.

The WPPSI has been compared in many research studies with other tests for concurrent validity. The manual reports correlations with two other intelligence tests: *Stanford-Binet* and *Pictorial Test of Intelligence* (PTI). Correlations with the *Binet* for the Verbal subtests ranged from .39 to .63, and with the PTI from .22 to .56. WPPSI Verbal IQ correlated .76 with the *Binet* IQ and .53 with the PTI.

Conclusions. This is a well-standardized test, though normative data are not available for visually impaired or blind children. Validity data are good, but test-retest data are needed by age level. Except for several of the first items on the Arithmetic subtest, no visual skills are needed to respond to the items on the Verbal Scale. Due to the emphasis on verbal skills, results of this scale must be carefully interpreted because verbal skills are likely to take longer to develop for young visually impaired and blind children. Results of the WPPSI may be an underestimate of the abilities of some of these children. For this reason, it is important to consider WPPSI results in light of a child's adaptive behaviors and language skills.

Criterion-Referenced Tests and Informal Measures

There are numerous criterion-referenced tests and informal measures available. The criteria used to select measures for review were that (a) the instrument had been published within the past 15 years (so that the content was appropriate), (b) the measure comprehensively assessed an area (to provide the type of detailed information necessary for programming decisions), and (c) the instrument did not require vision for most of the items. Checklists were not considered because of the cursory nature of the information obtained. Table 4 shows areas assessed by those tests and measures selected for review.

The test reviews that follow include an evaluation of the technical adequacy of the measures and descriptions of materials and administration procedures. When necessary, adaptations are suggested for tests that were not specifically designed for infants and young children with little or no vision.

TABLE 4
Criterion Tests and Informal Measures for Infants and Preschoolers

Tests	Areas Assessed by Subtests				
	Cognitive	Play	Motor	Adaptive	Speech and Language
Bayley Scales of Infant Development (2 to 30 months)				Behavior Record	
Brigance Diagnostic Inventory of Early Development (Birth through 6 years)	General Knowledge & Comprehension	Gross Motor (B-4 through B-13) Fine Motor (c-1, 2, 3 & C-7, 8, 9)	Pre-ambulatory Gross & Fine Motor	Self-Help	Prespeech & Speech and Language
Growing Up (Birth to 6 years)	Intellectual Development		Physical Development Fine Motor	Self-Help Skills Social Personal Development	Language Development
Informal Assessment of Developmental Skills (Infants and preschoolers)	Cognition		Psychomotor	Self-help Social-Emotional	Language
Ordinal Scales of Psychological Development (Birth to 2 years)	Any of the 7 scales are relevant	Most useful are Schemes, Objects in Space, and Causality			Vocal Imitation
Oregon Project for Visually Impaired & Blind Preschoolers (Birth to 6 years)	Cognitive	Fine Motor Gross Motor	Fine and Gross Motor	Self-Help and Socialization	Language

Bayley Scales of Infant Development
Infant Behavior Record

Author: Nancy Bayley

Publisher: The Psychological Corporation
555 Academic Court
San Antonio, TX 78204

Copyright: 1969

General Description. The Infant Behavior Record (IBR) is part of the *Bayley Scales of Infant Development,* but is not a part of the standardized test. Instead, this is a type of rating scale where ratings for each item can be compared to a table indicating the percent of children in an age group who received the same rating. The purpose of the IBR is to assess a child's "characteristic behavior patterns" (p. 99).

The only materials needed are the manual and record book. The IBR is to be completed by the examiner immediately after the administration of the Bayley Mental and Motor Scales. Thus, ratings are based on observation of a child's performance during testing with these scales. No adaptations are needed for visually impaired or blind children. One item requires rating the child's interest in sights-looking. This item could be left out of the ratings.

Description of Items. There are 30 items on the IBR. The first 15 items assess categories of behavior such as cooperativeness, fearfulness, activity, and general emotional tone. Most items are rated on a scale of 1 to 9, two have scales of 1 to 5, and two are scored yes or no. In addition, for eight of these items there are checklists for other related behaviors that were noted. Nine items deal with the child's degree of interest in sensory areas such as listening to sounds, body motion, and mouthing or sucking pacifier. Three items tap the degree of energy and coordination displayed; one item requires the examiner to rate the adequacy of the test as an indication of the child's characteristics; one requires noting any deviant behavior observed; and the last is a general evaluation of the child as normal or exceptional.

Technical Adequacy

Field Test or "Standardization." Frequencies in the table are based on data for 40 to 94 cases per age level. More than half of the age levels have fewer than 55 subjects. Most of the children were those who participated in the standardization of the entire *Bayley Scales*.

In the manual various "suggestive" findings of work with the IBR are discussed. The findings show that certain items seem to be related to cognitive performance and some items may discriminate between groups of "suspect" infants and normal infants. However, too little information is presented on the studies to draw any conclusions.

Reliability and Validity. No reliability or validity information is presented for the IBR.

Conclusions. The ratings on the IBR are based on subjective impressions of the examiner and should be interpreted as such. As an informal description of some of a child's social behaviors, the Record could be used as one source of information on adaptive behavior. Behaviors observed that could affect learning (in either a positive or negative way) would be useful note for planning an educational program. The IBR prompts an examiner to consider many important behaviors that might otherwise be overlooked; herein lies its strength.

Brigance Diagnostic Inventory of Early Development

Author: Albert Brigance

Publisher: Curriculum Associates
            5 Esquire Road
            North Billerica, MA 01862-2589

Copyright: 1978

General Description. This inventory is designed for children from birth through 6 years of age. Its purpose is to provide specific information for planning educational programs.

There are eleven sections that make up the test: Preambulatory Motor, Gross Motor, Fine Motor, Self-Help, Pre-Speech, Speech & Language, General Knowledge & Comprehension, Readiness, Basic Reading, Manuscript Writing, and Math.

The administration time can vary from 15 minutes to 2 hours depending on how much of the inventory is used. Administration procedures are clearly and concisely described in the manual.

Materials consist of the manual and a record book. Quite a few easily obtained toys and materials are needed. Examiners will need to plan ahead to be sure these items are available before testing. The author gives permission for duplication of pages needed for testing. No adaptations are suggested for children who are visually impaired or blind, but few are needed below the age of 3 years and many items usually learned by children between 3 and 7 years, do not require vision.

Description and Evaluation of Subtests

Preambulatory Motor Skills. The subtest contains 36 skills tested in supine, 14 in prone, 11 for sitting, and 16 for standing. This comprehensive section has pictorial sequences that are particularly useful for educating the parent in terms of what behaviors to teach and why. It is a good idea to test for the startle response late in the testing session because a baby may cry. Eight of the 36 items tested in supine require vision.

Gross Motor Skills. Skills tested include standing, walking, stairs, running, jumping, hopping, kicking, balance board, rolling and throwing, ball bouncing, rhythm, and wheel toys. A beeper ball could be used for children with little or no vision. Some of these skills could be part of an assessment of play skills.

Fine Motor Skills. This taps many skills used in kindergarten and preschool, but that are not usually found on other tests. Included are manipulative skills, block building, puzzles, prehandwriting, drawing, designs, cutting with scissors, painting with a brush, and clay. A number of these items require vision at the older age levels.

Self-Help Skills. In this section are 35 items that assess feeding and eating behaviors (from a sucking reflex to preparing a sandwich) and 45 that tap various dressing and undressing skills (from "cooperates in undressing" to "zips a back zipper"). There are 22 items to assess bathing and grooming, and 12 on toileting. An interesting series of 9 items assesses knowledge of household chores. This is particularly useful with visually impaired and blind children who need to learn the importance of order early in their lives to aid them in locating things. Items include remembering where objects are kept or belong and putting toys away.

Prespeech. For the three parts of this section, 11 items tap receptive language, 9 assess use of gestures, and 14 deal with vocalizations. Though important skills are considered in this section, to plan an effective program for children who are not yet talking, the information would need to be combined with information from the Vocal Imitation section of the *Ordinal Scales of Psychological Development* (Uzgiris & Hunt, 1975).

Speech and Language. This section assesses syntax with 22 items, social speech with 16 items, verbal directions with 15 items, ability to give personal data with 11 items, vocabulary (receptive and expressive) with 36 items, articulation of sounds with 15 items, memory with 14 items (words and numbers), and singing skills with 10 items.

General Knowledge and Comprehension. Many items on this section are verbal. Examples include 12 items on knowing where to go for services, 18 items for knowing use of objects, 12 items on function of community helpers, 12 items for knowing what to do in different situations, and 14 items dealing with time concepts such as "tonight" and "morning." Other subjects such as Classifying and Directional/Positional Concepts involve pictures and would need to be adapted by using objects instead. Though this section of the *Brigance Inventory* does not tap a large number of cognitive skills, the ones that are covered are worth considering. Nearly all of the subtests begin with items that are typically learned by children at the age of 3 years and up. Other than knowledge of body parts, this section of the inventory would not be appropriate for children less than 3 years of age.

Readiness. Eighteen items assess responses to books and many could be used with visually handicapped children (e.g., turns pages individually, wants to hear the same story repeated, and is interested in different kinds of stories). Remaining items in this section deal with letter knowledge and visual discrimination. Large print or braille adaptations could be made.

Basic Reading Skills. Auditory discrimination is not a reading skill, and hence these 26 items are misplaced under this section. The remaining items for this section deal with letter sounds and reading words and passages. Large print or braille adaptations would be necessary.

Manuscript Writing. This section would be most useful with children who have usable vision and are able to print or write in manuscript. Skills tested range from printing letters to writing simple sentences in manuscript.

Math. Item sequences that do not require vision are number concepts (counting quantities) and counting by rote. Addition and subtraction combinations could be given orally, and if real money were used some of the money recognition items could be given. Items dealing with recognizing and writing numbers might be given in large print or braille. The time items would require a braille clock for children with little or no vision.

It is important to note that when braille letters or numbers are used the type of discriminations required are different and sometimes more difficult than those required for printed letters and numbers.

Technical Adequacy

Field Testing. The inventory was extensively field tested in 16 states which resulted in revisions and additions of items, addition of reference material, and evaluation of the material to ensure that it was not prejudicial or stereotypic.

Reliability. No information is provided in this area.

Validity. The items were selected based on an extensive review of the developmental literature and other tests. Sources are cited. The inventory was critiqued by over 100 professionals in different types of programs.

Conclusions. This Inventory is comprehensive and well thought out. Many skills are assessed that are not usually covered by other tests. Test-retest and interrater reliability data are needed. The Prespeech section is the least thorough and would need to be supplemented as suggested. Most of the items for skills usually learned by children prior to 3 years of age require little if any adaptation and would be very helpful for program planning. Information would have to be interpreted in light of usual delays in development for visually impaired and blind children. Skills usually learned by children at 3 through 6 years of age require more adaptations, especially those testing early academic skills.

Growing Up: A Developmental Curriculum

Authors: Noel B. Croft and Lee W. Robinson

Publisher: Parent Consultants
201 Hardy Circle
Austin, Tx 78757

Copyright: 1984

General Description.   *Growing Up* is an outgrowth and an expansion of *Project Vision Up*, which was an informal assessment procedure with accompanying suggestions for remedial activities for visually impaired preschoolers. *Growing Up* is designed for use with children functioning at a level below that of 6-year-olds, and it can be used with normal children or children with mental and/or physical impairments. The purpose of *Growing Up* is to provide information for planning instructional programs.

The curriculum covers six areas of development: Physical Development, Fine Motor Development, Self-Help Skills, Social Personal Development, Language Development, and Intellectual Development. Each area is subdivided into "strands." For example, Self-Help Skills consists of strands such as eating, dressing, toileting, mobility, grooming, and sleeping.

The administration of the assessment component of the curriculum is unique. Parents of the child being assessed are given a set of cards and asked to sort them. Each card has a description of a particular skill printed on it. Parents sort the cards into three piles: one pile is for tasks their child can do, another is for tasks their child does not do, and the third is the "not sure" pile for tasks the child does sometimes. Sorting the cards for the six areas takes approximately 30 to 40 minutes. An alternative to using the cards is to use the skill descriptions presented in a book format. Both the cards and the pages of the book are color coded for each of the six areas.

Each skill listed on a card or in the book is coded with an approximate age level at which nonhandicapped children usually perform the skill. These age levels are based on information from a review of the literature and thus are only estimates. The purpose of the levels is more for sequencing the skills, and the ages cannot be used as normed scores. Each skill tested in *Growing Up* is also listed in one of three volumes that aid in planning remedial activities for areas of difficulty. Following the item is a behavioral description and several teaching activities for that skill. For many of the skills, sketches of children performing the skills are provided. These sketches would be helpful to use during assessment if parents are unsure of what correct performance of the skill should look like. Materials that would be helpful for teaching the skill are also listed. The pages in these three volumes are also color coded to correspond to the color for each of the six areas assessed with the cards or the book.

The materials for the curriculum consist of the Handbook-Index that describes the program, an Assessment Questionnaire for the examiner's use in planning and carrying out the assessment, a Profile Sheet for recording information on skills mastered, an Activity Record for recording performance once skills are selected for teaching, and the volumes that describe remedial activities and materials.

Description and Evaluation of Sections.   Parents are not required to sort through all of the cards in the curriculum. Instead, for each area the examiner is to ". . . provide the parents with enough cards with norms set above and below the child's chronological age to provide a complete assessment of strengths and weaknesses" (p. 14). This direction is somewhat subjective.

Physical Development. For this section there are 173 items. Skills range from lifting the head when in the prone position to making basic skipping motions.

Fine Motor Development. There are 159 items in this section. Skills tested range from demonstrating a grasping reflex to building creative structures with blocks.

Self-Help. Skills assessed in this section vary from opening mouth for a nipple to going to the store to spend money. There are 173 items included in this section.

Social-Personal Development. A rather detailed assessment of this area is provided by the 109 possible items. The range of skills is from exploratory play with paper to reacting emotionally to the death of a close family member or a pet. Included are several items related to the child's response to his or her handicap (e.g., "The child appears to accept his handicap and to adjust to it").

Language Development. There are 151 items on this section. Skills tapped range from birth cry to being able to describe details of short trips. Numerous items on articulation are involved.

Intellectual Development. This section consists of 140 items. The range of skills assessed is from following an object through a 180 degree arc to beginning to tell time using a clock. Whether all of these skills are relevant to later cognitive development is questionable.

Though a child could use vision for many items, the behaviors are often described in such a way that other modalities could be used instead.

Technical Adequacy

Field testing. No information is presented for field testing of the curriculum.

Validity. Item selection was based on a review of the child development literature and previous experience with *Project Vision Up*. The various resources and consultants used to develop *Growing Up* are listed in the Handbook-Index.

Though no data are presented for *Growing Up*, a study with 32 kindergarteners suggested the results of *Vision Up* were related to results obtained with the *Wechsler*, the *Bruinicks-Oseretsky Test of Motor Proficiency*, the *Vineland*, and the *Peabody Picture Vocabulary Scale* (Markland, 1979).

Reliability. A study with the earlier *Project Vision Up* (Wright, 1980) suggested high internal consistency reliability with parents sorting the cards.

No data are presented for test-retest reliability.

Conclusions. Given the subjective and informal nature of the administration of *Growing Up*, the fact that some skill descriptions are somewhat vague for parents to use in assessing their child, and the lack of information on technical adequacy of the asssessment procedure, results must be interpreted with a great deal of caution. This is indeed an informal assessment procedure, and results should be used accordingly. However, there seem to be three strengths of the *Growing Up* curriculum for assessing visually impaired and blind infants and preschoolers. First, the curriculum could be used as a supplement to information obtained from other more extensively developed measures. The Social-Personal Development section may be particularly useful for this purpose because it contains some items related to a child's response to his or her handicap that do not appear on other measures. Second, use of the sorting technique may be a way to help some parents become more active participants in the assessment process and help them become more aware of their child's skills. The third strength is the extensive amount of material provided that could be used to write remedial programs.

Informal Assessment of Developmental Skills for Visually Handicapped Students
Part Two: Informal Assessment of Developmental Skills for Younger Visually Handicapped and Multihandicapped Children

Authors: Rose-Marie Swallow, Sally Mangold,
            and Phillip Mangold

Publisher: American Foundation for the Blind
            15 West 16th Street
            New York, NY 10011

Copyright: 1978

General Description.   This series of checklists was developed to aid in assessing the special needs of infants and preschoolers who have little or no vision. Checklists were developed by teachers of visually handicapped students.

It is suggested that teaching objectives can be determined by noting the first behavior that is not in a child's repertoire for each section. There are five checklists: Self-Help, Psychomotor, Social-Emotional, Language, and Cognition.

Permission is given on page 2 to duplicate the checklists for "educational use with visually handicapped children."

Description of Checklists

Self-Help. The self-help areas assessed are: feeding, dressing, undressing, washing hands, grooming, and toileting. There are from 4 to 12 items per area. Examiners check the statement that best describes a child's performance. There are from 4 to 9 descriptions from which to choose for each item, and these descriptions are sequenced from beginning to advanced performance (e.g., "bottle feed" to "accepts and chews bite-sized pieces of solid food").

Psychomotor. For this checklist there are 28 gross motor items and 18 fine motor items. Locomotion and manipulation are emphasized because they are so important for visually impaired and blind students. Skills range from ability to make head movements to aquatic activities for the gross motor area. Included are items particularly important for children with little or no vision, such as the ability to open and close doors. Fine motor items range from reflexive grasping to use of scissors.

Social-Emotional. This checklist is particularly useful for preschoolers because this area is rarely assessed by other tests. Items assess the child's response to adults, to objects, and to other children. Self-confidence when playing and decision making are also considered. There are 14 items on the checklist, with from 3 to 9 possible descriptions of each behavior. Each item is checked as developed, in transition, or not present.

Language. This checklist taps nonverbal communication, imitation, receptive and expressive use of gestures or signs, fingerspelling, and verbal language. Pictures to use for communicating and some reading and writing items are also included. There are 19 items on the checklist. The *Ordinal Scales of Psychological Development* (reviewed later in this chapter) would provide a more comprehensive and detailed assessment of children who are not yet talking. For preschoolers, however, this checklist could be combined with the more comprehensive *Brigance Inventory of Early Development* (reviewed earlier) to assess unique aspects of communication such as use of signs or pictures.

Cognition. This checklist is based on the *Ordinal Scales*. It would be preferable to use the *Ordinal Scales* themselves, along with the supplementary manual by Dunst. These manuals are reviewed in detail later in this chapter. These manuals provide more detailed and comprehensive information.

Technical Adequacy. No data are provided on field testing, reliability, or validity of the checklists. Thus, results must be interpreted in light of the informal nature of the checklists.

Conclusions. These checklists could provide some useful information for planning programs for young visually impaired and blind children, particularly for preschoolers. The *Ordinal Scales* would be more useful for children less than 2 years of age. The Social-Emotional checklist should probably be used with any preschool child with little or no vision. Other available checklists and tests do not cover this area as well.

Ordinal Scales of Psychological Development

Authors: Ina Uzgiris and J. McVicor Hunt

Publisher: University of Illinois Press
            Box 5081, Station A
            54 Gregory Drive
            Champaign, IL 61820

Copyright: 1975

General Description.   The *Ordinal Scales* are based on Piaget's description of cognitive development from birth to 2 years of age (i.e., the sensorimotor period). Seven scales make up the test: Object Permanence, Means-Ends, Vocal Imitation, Gestural Imitation, Operational Causality, Construction of Objects in Space, and Schemes for Relating to Objects.

A good background in Piagetian theory is needed to correctly administer and interpret the *Scales*. This is particularly important when adaptations of items are made for visually impaired and blind children so that the intended skill is tested. Dunst (1980) has written a manual to accompany the *Scales*. In this manual, many items were added where gaps seemed to exist in the *Scales*, the administration procedures are more fully described, and a few items were changed. The protocol in the Dunst manual is especially useful. This manual also describes results of studies with the *Scales* and at-risk handicapped infants.

Any or all of the *Scales* can be used, but administration of the entire test would take about two hours.

The materials needed are the book for the *Ordinal Scales*, a record book, and easily obtained toys listed in the book. The manual by Dunst is also very helpful.

Items in each scale are organized in a hierarchy of development so that the item following the child's highest success would be the next appropriate skill to teach the child.

Description of Scales

Object Permanence. There are 14 items on the original scale and Dunst has added 7 items in his manual. This scale assesses a range of skills leading to the understanding that objects continue to exist even though they are no longer visually available. Skills progress from visual tracking to finding an object hidden under one of three screens. This scale requires vision, but some of the early items could be adapted by observing the child's tactile rather than visual search behavior.

Means-Ends. There are 13 items on the original scale and Dunst has added 12 items. This taps a child's problem solving behavior. Items progress from hand watching to using foresight by not trying to stack a solid circle on a post. Vision is required on many items, but about ⅓ of the items could be easily adapted. For example, one item uses some type of locomotion to obtain an object that is out-of-reach; a musical toy could be used to facilitate locating the toy.

Vocal Imitation. This is one of the most useful and important scales. There are 9 items on the original scale and Dunst added 6 items. This scale does not require vision. Items progress from "responds to voice" up to "imitation of novel words." This seems to be the most comprehensive and useful published scale to assess vocal behavior for children less than 2 years of age.

Gestural Imitation. The original scale contains 9 items and Dunst has added 8 items. The progression of skills on this scale is similar to that of Vocal Imitation except gestures are involved. Nearly all items require vision. The scale could be adapted by use of physical prompts (e.g., bang table with child's hand and see if child repeats behavior).

Operational Causality. The recognition of cause-and-effect relationships is assessed on this scale by 7 items on the original scale and an additonal 4 items added by Dunst. The recognition of cause and effect is important for sighted children and is particularly helpful for children with a visual impairment or who are blind. All but the hand watching item could be adapted for visually impaired and blind children. A clear understanding of Piagetian theory would be necessary to make the adaptations and ensure that the appropriate skills are tested. Skills range from "vocalizes/ smiles in response to adult talking" to "searches for causal mechanism" to "activates a wind-up toy."

Construction of Objects in Space. This scale taps the child's use of skills for relating objects in meaningful ways. There are 11 items on the original scale and 10 items added by Dunst. Items range from searching for sound with eyes to indicating the absence of familiar persons. Eleven items require vision, eight of which could be adapted. Play skills such as use of container and contained objects, building with blocks, and banging toys are involved.

Schemes for Relating Objects. Ten items make up the original scale and Dunst has added 6 items. This scale assesses the child's use of various sensorimotor skills with particular types of objects. Skills progress from mouthing to naming objects. Only one item requires vision. Useful play skills are tapped by this scale, Particularly for children under 12 months of age.

Technical Adequacy

Field testing. The original scale was field tested three times, and items were revised based on the results obtained. Dunst reports results of use of the *Scales* with 36 handicapped and at-risk infants.

Reliability. Dunst (1980) reports interrater reliability data from four studies with correlations ranging from .85 to .99. He also reports test-retest correlations from .88 to .96 from several studies using "short-term intervals."

Validity. Items were selected based on Piaget's description of cognitive development, thus there is a strong theoretical basis for the *Scales*. Items were sequenced on the basis of a logical analysis of how skills develop and which skills are prerequisites to others. Dunst (1980) obtained correlations ranging from .70 to .92 when examining the intercorrelations of the subtests.

Using his procedure for determining an "estimated developmental age," he found correlations ranging from .76 to .93 for subtests of the *Scales* and the Griffiths subtests. Estimated Mental Age from the *Scales* correlated .97 with the Griffith's Mental Age.

Data do not support long-term stability of performance (Dunst, 1982).

Numerous studies have examined Piaget's contention of the hierarchial progression of sensorimotor development, and there is considerable evidence to support this progression (Dunst, 1982). Patterns of development during the sensorimotor period have been found to be similar for sighted and blind infants (Dunst, 1980).

Conclusions. These *Scales* can provide useful information for planning educational programs for visually impaired and blind infants. Skills are assessed that are important for the development of cognition, language, and play behavior. Object Permanence, Means-Ends, and Gestural Imitation will be the least useful because of the visual requirements. Vocal Imitation requires no adaptation and provides detailed and comprehensive information for planning prespeech programs. Operational Causality will require adaptations made by someone with a good understanding of Piaget's theory so that appropriate skills are tested. Recognizing how to have an effect on things in the environment is an important cognitive skill for visually impaired and blind children. Construction of Objects in Space and Schemes for Relating Objects provide useful information on the development of cognition and play skills. Adaptation of several items is needed on Construction of Objects in Space and for one item for Schemes. This is a difficult test to learn, but well worth the effort required.

Oregon Project for Visually Impaired and Blind Preschoolers

Authors: Donnise Brown, Vickie Simmons,
               and Judy Methvin

Publisher: Jackson County Education Service District
             101 North Grape Street
             Medford, OR 97501

Copyright: 1979

General Description. This inventory was written for children from birth to 6 years of age. Its purpose is "to provide assessment and curriculum guidance to educators of young children with visual deficits" (p. 1).

Six developmental areas are assessed: Cognitive, Language, Self-Help, Socialization, Fine Motor, and Gross Motor.

Items on this unique inventory have been assigned one-year age levels appropriate for sighted children. However, skills that take a longer time for visually impaired and blind children to acquire are coded as such. Some items have special codes to indicate that they are additional skills that need to be learned because the child has a visual impairment or is blind (e.g., "Locates dropped object up to 8 feet away with sound cue"). One additional code indicates that an item may not be appropriate for a child who is totally blind.Special administration procedures for the Gross Motor items such as co-acting (acting in unison) are described when necessary so that the instructions are understood by the child.

Extensive recommendations are given in the manual for teaching each skill. The recommendations appear useful, are clearly written, and several alternatives are provided for each skill.

Information is obtained by interview, but items can be administered or directly observed. No specific procedures are described for administering items, and if this is done the examiner would have to be sure that the toys needed for infants and the materials needed for preschoolers are available. The toys needed are those usually available to children (e.g., blocks and puzzles). For older children, some braille letters and numbers may be necessary. Other than toys and braille letters and numbers, the only materials needed are the manual and a record book.

Because the Inventory was designed for visually impaired and blind children, any adaptations needed to test certain skills are indicated in the manual.

Description of Developmental Areas

Cognitive. There are 157 items in this section. Skills tested range from "Alerting to daily stimulation" to "Reading braille letters." Ten of the items may not be appropriate for a totally blind child.

Language. This area is composed of 130 items. Both receptive and expressive skills are tapped. Items range from "Alerts to a wide range of auditory stimulation" to "Changes word order appropriately to ask questions." Two of these items require some vision.

Self-Help. This area has 128 items, none of which require vision. Skills range from "Sucks and swallows liquid" to "Walks to school, playground, or store within two blocks of home independently."

Socialization. Eighty-seven items make up this area, 5 of which require some vision. The abilities assessed range from "Quiets or changes body movement in response to touch, sight or sound of familiar person" to "Explains relationship of family members ('Uncle Bob is Daddy's brother')."

Fine Motor. There are 94 items for this area, 21 of which require some vision. The first three items involve visual tracking, and the last item requires printing or brailling the numbers 1 to 10.

Gross Motor. None of the 99 items for this area require vision. The range of skills is from "Moves head to side while lying on back" to "Jumps rope by self (turning own rope)."

Technical Adequacy

Field testing. The inventory was field tested with 75 visually impaired children from Oregon and Arizona. Based on results of this field testing, items were clarified, added, deleted, and the placement of 25 items in the hierarchy was changed. The original version had 693 skills, and the present version has 695. A student profile to summarize performance was added, as were many teaching activities.

Reliability. No data are provided on reliability.

Validity. Items were developed based on a review of the current literature, records of children in the Southern Oregon Program for Visually Impaired, and input from preschool teachers for blind children. Input from "many professionals" in the field was also obtained.

Conclusions. This inventory is a very useful instrument for planning educational programs for both visually impaired and blind children. The fact that the inventory was designed with the special needs of these children in mind is certainly an asset. Test-retest and interrater relibility data are needed. A number of areas are not as comprehensive as the *Brigance Diagnostic Inventory of Early Development*. Hence, a combination of the two inventories would provide detailed and comprehensive information for planning programs, while at the same time circumventing vision problems and taking into consideration the special needs of these children. The inventory is not as thorough as the *Ordinal Scales* for children from birth to 12 months of age.

Assessment of the School-aged Child

The assessment of a school-aged child cannot be satisfactorily carried out with the administration of an intelligence test and one or two tests of achievement. The issues involved with a child's academic performance are very complex and require a thorough and well-planned approach. The information in this chapter covers general issues that deserve careful thought, special considerations needed in order to carry out a valid assessment, and detailed reviews of norm- and criterion-referenced tests and informal measures.

The Need for Order

It was noted earlier that visually impaired and blind preschoolers need to learn the importance of order (e.g., have a place for their toys). Learning to be orderly carries over to the school years as well. To function as efficiently as possible, a student with little or no vision will need to be organized and have specific places to keep various items. This will aid in locating objects and materials and will help avoid any unnecessary and frustrating search for things. Observation of the student's functioning in school and at home should include an evaluation of how orderly the environment is and how orderly the student is in these situations.

Overprotection

In trying to be helpful to a handicapped student, parents, teachers, and peers can do too much and actually interfere with the student's learning. A consideration of this factor is helpful when observing the student in school and at home. The student's safety is obviously of prime importance, but it must be realistically balanced with teaching the student to be as independent and as skilled as possible.

Time Limits on Tests

If possible, it is better to use tests for visually impaired and blind students that do not have timed items, otherwise the student will be penalized. If large print versions of tests are used, or some type of magnifying device is employed, more time will be needed on timed items. Even students with partial vision require more time to read the material than sighted students. If braille materials are used, considerably more time will be required. Kederis, Nolan, and Morris (1967) suggest that the average blind reader needs at least twice the time to cover materials as do sighted readers or listeners. Fatigue can certainly become a factor for these students during testing because of the time required to read the material.

Special Assessment Issues

Cognitive Assessment

Good judgment is particularly important in interpreting results of intelligence tests for visually impaired and blind students. This population of students is definitely heterogenous in terms of educational needs, hence each student will require a program designed to meet his or her unique situation.

Ashman (1982) suggests that to avoid overinterpreting test results for these students, the standard error of measurement should be used to describe a range of performance rather than reporting a single score. This is good practice to use when reporting results for any student, but is particularly important when handicapped students are tested.

Numerous studies have been carried out to examine any differences that might exist in WISC Verbal Scale profiles for visually impaired and blind students compared to sighted students. Results indicate that blind students score higher on Digit Span and lower on Similarities. This effect was found to be consistent across age levels from 7 through 11 years (Tillman & Osborne, 1969). Several other studies (Gilbert & Rubin, 1965; Hopkins & McGuire, 1966) have also found significantly high means on Information and low means on Comprehension for blind students. These authors suggest that including Digit Span as a subtest, and prorating scores based on results of all six subtests, results in spuriously high IQ scores. Tillman (1967) found that using this approach did yield a higher mean IQ for a group of 38 subjects. However, including the Digit Span subtest raised the mean IQ about as much as the Comprehension and Similarities subtests lowered it.

In a review of studies on the reliability of the WISC, Tillman (1973) found that internal consistency and test-retest coefficients were about the same for blind students as for sighted students. He noted that few studies have been done with blind students on the validity of the WISC. Questions exist regarding the appropriateness of the content for these students, and predictive validity studies are sorely needed.

Another issue to keep in mind when interpreting results of IQ tests is that for some visually impaired and blind children, abstract concepts tend to take longer to develop than for sighted students (Ashman, 1982).

If intelligence tests are to continue to be required in order to make decisions regarding eligibility for special education services, then there is certainly a need for a new test of intelligence. As Hopkins and McGuire (1966) point out, it would be desirable to have two sets of norms ". . . so that a blind child might not only be compared with those of like handicap, but also with those with whom he must compete in the academic and vocational world" (p. 73).

Achievement

When assessing achievement it is important to try to relate the testing to achievement goals in the classroom as much as possible. This is easier to

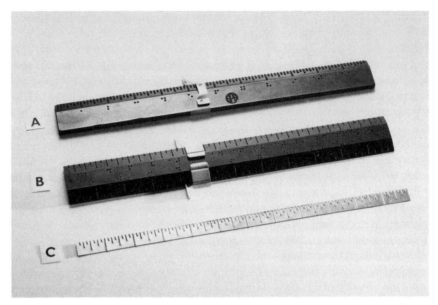

Figure 6. Braille rulers. (Courtesy the American Printing House for the Blind.)

do with criterion-referenced rather than norm-referenced tests because of the flexibility allowed in administration of the instruments. However, it is what is taught that needs to be tested.

One of the goals for achievement testing is to determine a child's strengths and areas of difficulty. In order to do this, any adaptive devices and materials used in the classroom will need to used during the assessment. Examples include braille rulers, clocks, watches, and graphs. Students who know how to use an abacus could use this device on tests of arithmetic that allow sighted students to write out their computations. Figure 6 displays braille rulers. If an adventitiously blind student knows how to write, then paper with embossed lines could be used for testing spelling. This paper, or paper with heavy black lines, could be helpful for visually impaired students when assessing written expression. The use of a typewriter, low vision aids, or closed circuit TV systems may also aid a student in responding to test items.

Some standardized achievement tests have been modified in various ways for students with little or no vision. Because reading rates for braille are slower, the time limits on timed tests have often been extended. This may result in inflated scores (Ozias, 1975). When material is too visually detailed to translate (e.g., maps or graphs), or when it is not appropriate for students with little or no vision, the material is sometimes omitted. This procedure essentially gives the student credit for these items, but at least the student is not penalized (B. Duckworth, American Printing House for the Blind, personal communication, November, 1984).

No achievement tests have been standardized on visually impaired and blind students. Instead, some individually-administered tests have been transcribed into large print and braille (e.g., WRAT and *Keymath*). Unfortunately, these tests have serious problems with technical adequacy even for sighted students. (Detailed information is provided in the reviews that follow.) Some group-administered tests have also been transcribed into large print and braille, but individually-administered tests are needed for making decisions regarding eligibility for special education services. However, one group-administered test, the *Stanford Achievement Test* (SAT) (Madden, Gardner, Rudman, Karlsen, & Merwin, 1973), deserves special consideration. First, as Salvia and Ysseldyke (1981, p. 168) note, the "standardization, reliability, and validity are exceptionally good." Though it was not standardized on students with little or no vision, the SAT is the only achievement test with norm tables that have been adapted for these students. The combination of the SAT (grades 2.5 to 9.9) and the upward extension, the *Tests of Academic Skills* (TASK) (grades 8.0 through 13), provides achievement measures for grades 2.5 through 13. Braille and large print versions of the SAT and TASK are available from the American Printing House for the Blind. The subtests of the SAT vary depending on the level used. The subtests are Vocabulary, Reading Comprehension, Word Study Skills, Mathematics Concepts, Mathematics Computation, Mathematics Applications, Spelling, Language, Social Science, Science, and Listening Comprehension. TASK taps the areas of Reading, English, and Mathematics. Reviews are not included for these tests because they are group administered. However, the SAT and TASK could be used to obtain information that would be helpful for program planning. The scores could serve as one source of information to supplement data obtained from less technically adequate, but individually-administered, tests that are available in large print and braille.

When assessing the oral language of a young school-age student with little or no vision, several of the issues noted for assessing language of preschoolers are relevant. The use of personal pronouns may be delayed (Fewell, 1983; Goldman & Duda, 1978). The use of possessive pronouns such as *her* and *their* may also take longer to learn (Brown et al., 1979). Position concepts such as *up* and *right* are particularly important for these children. Hence, it is beneficial to be sure these concepts are clearly understood.

Adaptive Behavior. Vander Kolk (1981) notes that blind students consistently receive lower scores than sighted students on tests that assess social behavior. Thus, for junior high and high school students assessment of these skills can be particularly helpful.

If a visually impaired or blind student uses adaptive devices to carry out self-care and household tasks, these should be used when scoring items and they should be included in program planning. Examples include kitchen equipment such as knives with slicing guides and adapted measuring devices, braille clocks and watches, and tools that can be used by persons without vision.

Critical adaptive behaviors for visually impaired and blind students are those related to orientation and mobility. As Ashman (1982, p. 11) notes, "Minimal ability to get around in a public school setting is often misinterpreted as amazingly good by public school staff unfamiliar with the performance of the well trained blind individual. Intensive individual instruction in this area contributes strikingly to the blind child's independent functioning and social acceptability, as well as to positive self-concept." The input of an orientation and mobility instructor can be extremely helpful, if such services are available.

Because students may function differently in the more familiar home environment than in the school setting, it is a good idea to have both the teacher and the parents complete an adaptive behavior measure. If differences exist, they could be a function of the perspectives of different informants, or real differences in performance could be reflected. Follow-up on any differences in the reports could provide useful information for program planning.

Norm-Referenced Tests

Tests were reviewed if they were (a) designed to be individually administered (to meet legal requirements for special education eligibility decisions), (b) had been published within the last 15 years (so that content and norms were reasonably current), and (c) required responses that would circumvent a visual problem (so that students would have the enabling behaviors necessary for the test). If a test required vision on some items, but included a relatively large number of visually impaired and blind students in the sample, it was included. One exception to these criteria is the *Wechsler Preschool and Primary Scale of Intelligence* (Wechsler, 1967), which is more than 15 years old. It was included because the test options for assessing cognitive development are so limited for 5 and 6 year olds that this test often must be given consideration.

As with younger children, many school-age, visually impaired students with good usable vision can be tested with instruments for sighted children. In some cases magnification devices or enlargement of test materials, special lighting, and other special procedures may be required.

The *Perkins-Binet Test of Intelligence for the Blind* (Davis, 1980) is mentioned frequently in the literature. It was not reviewed because it has been withdrawn from the market and may be reissued pending major revisions and further research (Perkins School for the Blind, personal communication, November, 1984).

Following are detailed reviews of norm-referenced tests. The evaluation of the technical adequacy of these measures is based on the criteria presented in Chapter 1. Descriptions of administration and scoring procedures, materials, and types of responses required are included. Adaptations of some items for tests not designed for students with little or no vision are also suggested. See Table 5 for a summary of areas assessed for each of the norm-referenced tests reviewed.

Basic School Skills Inventory–Diagnostic

(See critique in Chapter 4.)

Battelle Developmental Inventory

(See critique in Chapter 4.)

Blind Learning Aptitude Test

Author: T. Ernest Newland

Publisher: University of Illinois Press
            Box 5081, Station A
            Champaign, IL 61820

Copyright: 1971

General Description.   The *Blind Learning Aptitude Test* (BLAT) was planned for students from 6 to 16 years of age to measure learning potential. However, it is suggested in the manual that it discriminates best for ages 6 through 12.

The 49 items tap six series of skills for which there are two practice items for each series. Though the BLAT does not have subtests, each series of items assesses a different skill.

Results are expressed in terms of Learning Quotients with a mean of 100 and standard deviation of 15. It is also possible to report a Test Age.

TABLE 5
Norm-Referenced Tests for Visually Impaired and Blind School-Age Students

Tests	Cognitive	Achievement	Adaptive	Language
		Areas Assessed		
Basic School Skills Inventory–Diagnostic (4 to 6 years, 11 months)			X	X
Battelle Developmental Inventory (Birth through 8 years)	X		X	X
Blind Learning Aptitude Test (6 to 16 years)	X			
Carrow Elicited Language Inventory (3 to 7 years, 11 months)				X
Detroit Tests of Learning Aptitude (6 through 17 years)	X			
KeyMath Diagnostic Arithmetic Test (Kindergarten through grade 6)		X		
Stanford Achievement Test * (Grades 2.5 to 9.9)		X		
Stanford–Binet Intelligence Scale	X			
Tactile Test of Basic Concepts (Kindergarten through grade 2)				X

The BLAT must be given individually and requires 20 to 45 minutes to administer.

Materials include the manual, a response sheet, and a set of plastic sheets containing figures in bas-relief form.

Description of Skills Tested. No knowledge of braille is required to interpret the figures on the plastic sheets. The figures are relatively large, so no fine discriminations are required. A student may make a verbal

TABLE 5 Continued

Tests	Areas Assessed			
	Cognitive	Achievement	Adaptive	Language
Test of Achievement Skills* (Grades 8 through 13)		X		
Test of Adolescent Language (11 years to 18 years, 5 months)				X
Test of Language Development–Intermediate (8 years, 6 months to 12 years, 11 months)				X
Test of Language Development– Primary (4 to 8 years, 11 months)				X
Vineland Social Maturity Scale (Birth to 18 years, 11 months)			X	
Wechsler Adult Intelligence Scale–Revised (16 years and up)	X			
Wechsler Intelligence Scale for Children–Revised (6½ through 16½ years)	X			
Wechsler Preschool and Primary Scale of Intelligence (4 to 6½ years)	X			
Wide Range Achievement Test (5 years and up)		X		

*Group administered test (see description under Achievement).

response to answer a question, but a pointing response is acceptable for all items. Tactile discrimination is required for all items.

The first series of 8 items requires finding the figure that is "not like the others." Classification skills are tapped.

The second series has 7 items where the student has to choose a figure from several on the page that matches a model figure. These items assess the ability to match-to-sample.

The third series of 6 items requires choosing the figure needed to complete a progression (e.g., a series of figures that increases in size). The student is given several figures from which to choose. Seriation or sequencing is required.

There are 16 items for the fourth series. The student must select from several figures the one that goes with another figure, so that the pair of figures goes together in the same way that another pair of figures goes together. The ability to determine analogous relationships is assessed.

Five items make up the fifth series. On these items the student selects from several figures the one that is needed to complete an incomplete figure. Knowledge of part-whole relationships is needed.

The last series consists of 7 items. The student is presented with a matrix of several figures with one missing. The task is to choose the missing figure from several alternatives. Pattern completion (i.e., recognition of the relationship between the figures and the use of the relationship rule to determine what figure would come next) is required.

The test is not timed which is helpful for visually impaired and blind students.

Technical Adequacy

Standardization. There were 961 students in the sample from age 6 through 21. However, norm tables only go up through age 16. The number of students for ages 6 through 16 varies from 19 to 106. Only at ages 10 and 14 do the numbers come close to 100 per level. Hence, the number of subjects per age level was too small to provide an adequate sample. The students were drawn from 12 states that were from the four regions of the country, but proportions do not correspond to census data. There were 446 girls and 515 boys. The sample closely approximated the 1966 data in the *Statistical Abstracts of the United States* in terms of white and non-white students. This was also true for comparison with the 1960 data in the Statistical Abstracts for occupational level for most of the occupational categories for the BLAT. No data are given for urban-rural residence. Seventy-nine percent of the students (760) were from residential schools and 201 were from day school programs. This is not representative of today's population of students who are primarily enrolled in public school programs. Hence, there are problems with the representativeness of the sample.

Reliability. A seven-month interval was used to assess test-retest reliability with 93 students 10 to 16 years of age. A correlation of .87 was obtained. Also, correlations were obtained for 24 students 6 to 10 years old ($r = .87$) and for 53 students 12 to 16 years old ($r = .90$), and no difference was suggested between the age levels. However, data are not given by age level.

A correlation of .93 was obtained for internal consistency.

Validity. The content validity of the BLAT might be questioned. The manual indicates that the test assesses processes or operations needed for learning. The ideas for the majority of items were from "culture free" tests for sighted students (e.g., *Kulman-Anderson, Culture Free Intelligence Test*) to minimize the effects of acculturation.

Concurrent validity data were obtained with the *Hayes-Binet* and the *WISC Verbal Scale*. With the *Hayes-Binet* the correlation for 663 students was .74; for 552 students and the *WISC* Verbal Scale the correlation was .71. The BLAT was also compared to results of an achievement test, the *Stanford Achievement Test*. Correlations ranged from .39 to .75.

Conclusions. An insufficient sample size was used for all but two age levels. Though the sample appears to be representative in terms of sex, race, and occupational level, it is not a geographically representative sample and no data are given for urban-rural residence. Further, 79% were from residential schools although today the vast majority of visually impaired and blind students are in public school programs.

Though test-retest data are encouraging, they are needed according to age level.

Though the BLAT could be used as one source of norm-referenced information on cognitive development, it would have to be supplemented with data from other sources that require responses other than tactile discrimination. The technical limitations of the test make it necessary to be cautious about interpreting results.

Carrow Elicited Language Inventory

(See critique in Chapter 4.)

Detroit Tests of Learning Aptitude

Author: Donald D. Hammill

Publisher: PRO-ED
5341 Industrial Oaks Blvd.
Austin, TX 78735

Copyright: 1985

General Description. The *Detroit Tests of Learning Aptitude* (DTLA) were designed for students who are 6 through 17 years of age. The three purposes of the DTLA are: (a) to inventory ". . . a person's relative strengths and weaknesses," (b) ". . . to obtain information that is helpful in identifying those children and young adults who are markedly deficient in intellectual ability" (p. 11), and (c) to use as a research tool to examine students' intellectual functioning.

There are 11 subtests that make up the DTLA: Word Opposites, Sentence Imitation, Oral Directions, Word Sequences, Story Construction, Design Reproduction, Object Sequences, Symbolic Relations, Conceptual Matching, Word Fragments, and Letter Sequences. Three of the subtests do not require vision (Word Opposites, Sentence Imitation, and Word Sequences). Hence, these three will be reviewed. The remaining eight subtests would be difficult to use with visually impaired students unless some of the materials were enlarged. Even then the pictures and some of the figures may be visually too complex for these students.

Results can be expressed in terms of percentiles and standard scores (mean = 10, s.d. = 3) for the subtests and quotients (mean = 100, s.d. = 15) for the composites (different combinations of the subtests). No composite scores can be determined for the three subtests that do not require vision.

Administration time for the entire test can vary from 50 minutes to 2 hours. Use of the three subtests that do not require vision would require approximately 15 to 30 minutes. Practice items are included for each subtest.

Description of Subtests. Following are reviews of the three subtests that could be used with blind and visually impaired students without modification.

Word Opposites. There are 50 possible items on this subtest for which the examiner states a word and the student is asked to give an opposite word. The words range in difficulty from "hot" to "former" and "tentative." This taps a student's vocabulary.

Sentence Imitation. Thirty possible items make up this subtest. The examiner orally presents a sentence and the student must repeat it exactly as it was stated. Examples of errors are incorrect word order, substitutions, contractions, and insertions. Speech impediments are ignored in scoring. The number of words per sentence range from 6 to 19 words. Assessed is "rote sequential memory that is highly influenced by competence in using standard English grammar" (p. 56).

Word Sequences. There are 30 possible items on this subtest for which the examiner repeats a series of unrelated single-syllable words. The student's task is to repeat the sequence in the correct order. An example of a sequence is "ear pig skate rope wool." The number of words varies from 3 to 8. This taps "short-term verbal memory and attention" (p. 56).

Technical Adequacy

Standardization. There were from 91 to 184 sighted subjects involved per age level. The demographic characteristics of the sample closely approximate the characteristics of the U.S. population in terms of sex, race, geographic area and urban/rural residence. No data are provided on the occupational levels of parents, but their educational levels are described.

Reliability. Test-retest data are given for 33 students (ages 6 through 17). Because of the restricted range (few low- and high-functioning students), a correction formula was used to assess reliability. Correlations were .91 for Word Opposites, .82 for Sentence Imitation, and .85 for Word Sequences. A two-week interval was used. Data are not presented by age level.

Standard errors of measurement are provided for each subtest by age intervals (e.g., 6/7 and 8/9).

Internal consistency coefficients for Word Opposites range from .87 to .93, for Sentence Imitation from .84 to .90, and for Word Sequences from .83 to .90.

Validity. Item analysis indicated that 77% of the median item difficulty percentages ranged between 15 and 85. Further, in terms of discriminating power, 79% of the coefficients reached or exceeded .3. In addition, for content validity, the subtests and composites fit with the models of intelligence that are "currently popular" (p. 80). They are also consistent with results of a survey of the "contents of currently used tests in print" (p. 80).

For criterion-related validity, the DTLA was compared to the WISC–R and the PPVT for 78 special education students. For the WISC–R, correlations with the DTLA subtests that do not require vision ranged from .49 to .76. The correlations of these subtests with the PPVT ranged from .58 to .70.

In terms of construct validity, DTLA results were examined for their relationship to age, achievement, subtest intercorrelation, and group differentiation. Correlations for age ranged from .42 to .68 (Md. 54). Correlations were obtained for results of the DTLA and the SRA Achievement Series for 25 second graders, 32 sixth graders, and 20 eleventh graders. Correlations for subtests not requiring vision ranged from nonsignificant to .67 at grade 2, from .35 to .91 at grade 6, and from nonsignificant to .89 at grade 11.

Intercorrelations of these three subtests ranged from .36 to .69. Subtest standard scores on the DTLA for 12 students "known to have low aptitude for school work" (p. 84) ranged from 5 to 8 and their mean General Intelligence Quotient was 75. This suggests that the DTLA was able to yield scores for these students that indicated that they were different from normal students.

Conclusions. The three subtests of the DTLA that do not require vision could provide useful supplemental information to results from other tests of intelligence where the entire test can be used. Except for the lack of data on socioeconomic level, the standardization is excellent. The reliability data are good, though additional test-retest data by age levels are desirable. A great deal of thought went into the construction of the test, and the validity data provided thus far are comprehensive and encouraging. It would appear to be worth the relatively small amount of time needed to administer these subtests to blind and visually impaired students in order to have the additional information the DTLA could provide. Given the problems noted for other tests of intelligence for these students, this additional information could be helpful. Cognitive skills assessed by these subtests are primarily short-term auditory memory, attention, vocabulary, and to some extent grammar.

KeyMath Diagnostic Arithmetic Test

Authors: **Austin Connolly, William Nachtman, and**
             E. Milo Pritchett

Publisher: **American Guidance Service**
             Publishers Building
             Circle Pines, MN 55014

Braille   **American Printing House for the Blind**
Version: **1839 Frankfort Ave.**
             P.O. Box 6085
             Louisville, KY 40206

Copyright: **1971, 1976**

General Description. This test is intended primarily for children from kindergarten through grade six. Though the *KeyMath* requires vision, there is a braille version of the test available through the American Printing House for the Blind. The items and technical data are essentially the same for both versions of the test. The braille version was not restandardized; it is simply a braille transcription.

The *KeyMath* is made up of 14 subtests divided into three areas: Content, Operations, and Applications.

A grade level score can be obtained for the total test only. No subtest scores can be obtained (American Guidance Service, personal communication, December, 1983).

Administration time is about 30 minutes for the regular version, but about an hour will be required for the braille edition. The test is not timed.

Materials needed are the manual, supplemental instructions for the braille version, the braille transcription of the cards for the items, the regular record book, and whatever equipment or material the student typically uses for arithmetic computation (except an electric calculator). Because the illustrations of money were eliminated on the braille version, real money is used for these items. Quantities needed are: 2 $1 bills, 1 half-dollar, 3 quarters, 4 dimes, 4 nickels, and 6 pennies. This totals $3.91.

It should be noted that though the *KeyMath* is described as a "criterion-referenced scale" (p. 2), there are insufficient items per area to use the test for this purpose.

Description of Areas Tested

Content. This area is composed of three subtests: Numeration with 24 items, Fractions with 11 items, and Geometry and Symbols with 20 items.

Operations. Six subtests make up this area. Four tap the basic operations: Addition, Subtraction, Multiplication, and Division. The other two subtests are Mental Computation and Numerical Reasoning.

Applications. The Word Problems subtest involves story problems to which the student gives an oral response. Missing Elements contains 7 items where the student must determine what element of the problem is missing and is needed to solve the problem. Money, Measurement, and Time are the last three subtests.

Technical Adequacy

Standardization. A total of 1,222 subjects participated in the standardization. Though the students were drawn from eight states, it was not a geographically representative sample (e.g., no southern states participated). No data are provided on socioeconomic status or sex. Race and community size were compared to the 1970 census data and though the demographic characteristics were fairly similar, the authors felt it was necessary to weight the proportions before calculating grade equivalents. Hence, the *KeyMath* normative sample cannot be considered representative of the U.S. population. Furthermore, because "item-sampling" was used, each student in the sample took only five of the test items. This approach ignores the fact that variables such as fatigue and persistence could affect performance.

Reliability. No test-retest data are given. Internal consistency correlations for the total score ranged from .94 to .97; for subtests the range is .23 to .90.

Standard errors of measurement are provided by grade level.

Validity. Item selection was based on review of 10 major mathematics programs and item assessment with data from 3,000 students.

No concurrent validity information is given in the manual for the present version of the test.

Conclusions. The sample for the *KeyMath* is not geographically representative, and the item sampling procedure ignores issues of fatigue and persistence. With no data on sex and socioeconomic status the representativeness of the same is questionable.

Though the other reliability data are good, the lack of test-retest data is a serious problem.

There are an insufficient number of items per skill to use the test for program planning, but some useful general information regarding areas of strength and difficulty could be obtained.

Stanford-Binet Intelligence Scale

(Information is not yet available on the Fourth Edition of the test for review. See the summary included under Cognitive Development in Chapter 4.)

Tactile Test of Basic Concepts

Author: Hilda R. Caton

Publisher: American Printing House for the Blind
            1839 Frankfort Ave.
            P.O. Box 6085
            Louisville, KY 40206

Copyright: 1967, 1970, 1971 (Boehm), 1976 (Caton)

General Description. This is the tactile analog to the *Boehm Test of Basic Concepts* (Boehm, 1971). It can be used with children from kindergarten through second grade. The purpose according to the Boehm (1971) manual is to assess a child's understanding of ". . . concepts basic to understanding directions and other oral communications from teachers at the

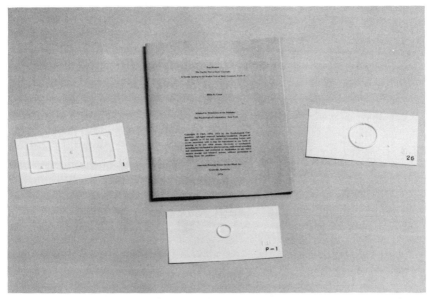

Figure 7. Raised line drawings. (Courtesy the American Printing House for the Blind.)

preschool and primary grade level" (p. 29). The *Tactile Test of Basic Concepts* (TTBC) is designed for use with children who need braille or other tactile media.

There are no subtests; rather, the TTBC consists of 50 items. Each of the 50 concepts is tested by using a raised line drawing on a plastic card. The same concepts are tested in the same order as on the *Boehm Test of Basic Concepts* (BTBC). When possible, simple geometric forms rather than detailed pictures are used to test the concept. If detailed drawings had been used, these would have been difficult for young blind children to interpret (Caton, 1976). Figure 7 displays these forms.

Scores are in the form of percent passing each item by grade and by socioeconomic level. Percentiles are also available by grade.

The test can be administered in one or two sessions, though one is usually sufficient. There are five practice cards to ensure that the directions are understood.

Materials include the manual, a scoring form, and 50 plastic TTBC cards.

Technical Adequacy.   Because the norm tables from the BTBC are used for the TTBC, the technical aspects of this test will be reviewed first. There are two forms (A and B) of the BTBC. The TTBC is based on Form A, so only this form will be reviewed.

Standardization (BTBC). The manual states that the BTBC was planned as ". . . a screening and teaching instrument rather than for predictive or administrative purposes" (p. 19). Hence, a representative national sample was not employed. The data are from responses of sighted children. Norms for beginning of the year were based on data from 3,517 kindergartners, 4,659 first graders, and 1,561 second graders. Midyear norms represent 865 kindergartners, 991 first graders, and 813 second graders. Children were tested from states from all four regions of the country, but proportions do not correspond to census data. Children were described as low, middle, or high socioeconomic level based on "the judgment of administrative personnel" (p. 19). Thus, the accuracy of these categories is questionable. No other demographic data are presented. The data in the norm tables cannot be considered representative. The author suggests collecting local data. This information would be more useful than the norm tables.

Reliability (BTBC). No test-retest data are given. Split-half reliability coefficients range from .68 to .90.

Standard errors of measurement are presented for all grade levels and by socioeconomic level.

Validity (BTBC). The only evidence of validity presented in the manual is that items were selected based on a review of curricular materials at preschool and primary grade levels for reading, arithmetic, and science. Words were selected that appeared frequently, that were rarely if ever defined, and that were relatively abstract.

Field Testing (TTBC). For the field testing, 75 blind students participated (25 from each of the three grade levels). The students were from six residential schools and six public day schools. From these data it was determined that students who were older, had been in school longer, and were in higher grades performed slightly better. Blind students in public school programs had performance that was slightly higher than those in residential programs. It was also noted that blind children had the most difficulty with concepts involving comparative judgments (e.g., middle, least), and they had the least difficulty with concepts where the child uses himself/herself as a referent (e.g., behind, away from). Comparison of performance by grade level revealed that blind children appear to learn these concepts as they progress through school.

Reliability (TTBC). No test-retest data were reported. These data are desirable even for an informal measure. The correlation for internal consistency was .87.

Standard error of measurement is reported but not by grade level.

Validity (TTBC). No significant differences were found in performance for blind children on the TTBC and sighted children on the BTBC. Data from the 75 blind children in the field testing were compared to the norms on the BTBC to obtain this information.

Conclusions. Because of the lack of demographic data on the sample, the fact that it was not geographically representative, and the lack of test-retest data, the test cannot be used as a norm-referenced test. However, if local normative data were collected, this would be useful.

Though the items appear to be important for success in the classroom, insufficient information is given in the manual to support the content validity of the test.

Because concept development is so important for the effective functioning of visually impaired and blind children, and because these concepts are more difficult to acquire if vision is impaired, the TTBC would seem to be helpful in any assessment of young elementary-aged students. Certainly the research that has been done on the TTBC suggests its relevance. Until more data are available on its technical adequacy, the TTBC is best used to obtain information for program planning.

Test of Adolescent Language

Authors: Donald Hammill, Virginia Brown, Steven Larsen, and
             J. Lee Wiederholt

Publisher: PRO-ED
             5341 Industrial Oaks Blvd.
             Austin, TX 78735

Copyright: 1980

General Description. This battery of tests was designed for students between the ages of 11 and 18-5. The *Test of Adolescent Language* (TOAL) assesses skills in listening, speaking, reading, and writing. Only the Speaking section and one part of the Writing section will be reviewed because these are the only parts that do not require vision.

The Speaking section is composed of two subtests: Speaking Vocabulary and Speaking Grammar. The Writing Vocabulary subtest could be used with students with little or no vision and who can use a brailler, typewriter, or who can write.

Results can be reported as scaled scores (mean of 10, standard deviation of 3) for subtests. Results of both subtests for speaking can be combined to obtain a Language Quotient for speaking.

Administration time for Speaking Vocabulary (SV) is 5 to 15 minutes and for Speaking Grammar (SG) 5 to 20 minutes. For sighted students

Writing Vocabulary (WV) takes from 10 to 25 minutes. More time would be required for this subtest for visually impaired or blind students.

Materials needed for the SV and SG subtests are the manual, a profile sheet, and an answer booklet. For the WV subtest, a brailler, typewriter, or paper would also be needed.

Description of Subtests

Speaking Vocabulary. This is a 20-item subtest where the examiner says a word and the student is asked to use the word in a sentence. Examples of words are "latch" and "hindrance."

Speaking Grammar. There are 24 items on this subtest for which the examiner verbally presents a sentence and the student must repeat it exactly. Though the student must recall what was said, results probably reflect syntactic abilities more than memory because with long sentences ". . . students have to fall back on their knowledge of syntax to help facilitate their memory of the sentence" (p. 11). An example of an item is "It isn't good for these two to eat so much."

Writing Vocabulary. For this subtest the examiner could read the vocabulary word to a student with little or no vision instead of asking the student to read the word. The student could then "write" a sentence using the word. Examples of words on this subtest are "solitary" and "gaunt." There are 24 items that make up this subtest.

Technical Adequacy

Standardization. A total of 2,723 participated in the standardization with at least 279 students per grade level. Though students were drawn from 17 states (including states from each of the four geographic regions) and three Canadian provinces, no data are given to demonstrate correspondence with census data. The sample does correspond closely to 1977 census data in terms of sex and urban-rural residence. No data are presented to describe the sample in terms of race or socioeconomic level.

Reliability. Test-retest data were obtained for 52 parochial school students from 11 through 14 years of age. A two-week retest interval was employed. For Speaking Vocabulary the correlation was .85, for Speaking Grammar .79, for the Speaking Quotient .85, and for Writing Vocabulary .90. The Speaking Vocabulary subtest, the Speaking Quotient, and the Writing Vocabulary subtest are sufficiently reliable to use in making placement decisions. However, data are needed by age level.

Internal consistency was assessed by grade level. The correlations for Speaking Vocabulary ranged from .7 to .9, for Speaking Grammar from .6 to .8, for the combined Spoken Language from .8 to .9, and for Writing Vocabulary from .6 to .9.

Interscorer reliability was assessed for Speaking Vocabulary and Writing Vocabulary, which involve some subjective evaluation (Speaking Grammar is objectively scored). For Speaking Vocabulary, the mean correlation was .96 and for Writing Vocabulary .87.

Standard errors of measurement are given by grade level for each subtest, each composite score, and the total score.

Validity. With regard to content validity, an extensive rationale is given for item selection and format based on a review of the research on language and on field testing with TOAL. Further, items were selected that fell within a range of 15% to 85% for item difficulty, and the items were shown to have acceptable discriminating power.

Results of the TOAL were compared for criterion-related validity to the *Peabody Picture Vocabulary Test* (PPVT), the Memory for Related Syllables from the *Detroit Tests of Learning Abilities* (DTLA), Reading and Language totals from the *Comprehensive Test of Basic Skills* (CTBS), and the Total Score for the *Test of Written Language* (TOWL). The following correlations were obtained for the Speaking Vocabulary: .73 for PPTV, .40 for DTLA, .55 for CTBS Reading, nonsignificant for CTBS Writing, and .57 for TOWL. Correlations for Speaking Grammar were: nonsignificant for PPVT, .49 for DTLA, nonsignificant for CTBS Reading, nonsignificant for CTBS Writing, and nonsignificant for TOWL. Writing Vocabulary coefficients were: .45 for PPVT, nonsignificant for DTLA, .63 for CTBS Reading, .44 for CTBC Writing, and .41 for TOWL. For the Spoken Language Quotient correlations were: .67 for PPVT, .60 for DTLA, .69 for CTBS Reading, .53 for CTBS Language, and .63 for TOWL.

In terms of construct validity, the mean scores of the TOAL increase with age. Subtest intercorrelations range from .32 to .75. The TOAL was shown to discriminate between a group of mentally retarded students and a hypothetical normal group, and between a group of LD students and the hypothetical normal group. Both mentally retarded and LD students make up groups which are likely to have language problems.

Conclusions. Demographic data are needed on the TOAL for race and socioeconomic status. The other factors appear to be adequate.

Internal consistency and interrater reliability data are good. Test-retest data provided are also good, but such information is needed by age level.

The validity of the TOAL appears to be sound.

Though the entire test cannot be used with students with little or no vision, the three subtests that can be used (i.e., Speaking Vocabulary, Speaking Grammar, and Writing Vocabulary) would provide useful information on language abilities.

Test of Language Development–Intermediate

Authors: Donald D. Hammill and Phyllis L. Newcomer

Publisher: PRO-ED
            5341 Industrial Oaks Blvd.
            Austin, TX 78735

Copyright: 1982

General Description. The *Test of Language Development–Intermediate* (TOLD–I) was planned for students who are between the ages of 8-6 and 12-11. The TOLD–I is made up of five subtests to provide a comprehensive assessment of language skills. None of the subtests require vision, thus the entire test can be used with children who are visually impaired or blind.

Percentiles and standard scores (mean = 10, standard deviation = 3) can be obtained for subtests. Quotients can be determined for composites which are combinations of subtests for Overall Spoken Language, Listening, Speaking, Semantics, and Syntax. The subtests are Sentence Combining, Characteristics, Word Ordering, Generals, and Grammatic Comprehension.

The TOLD–I is not timed. To administer the test takes about 30 to 45 minutes.

Materials needed include the manual and a record book.

Description of Subtests

Sentence Combining. This subtest contains 25 items. The examiner reads two or more simple sentences, and the student must combine these into a compound or complex sentence. This assesses a student's expressive syntactic abilities. An example of an item dictated by the examiner is "I like milk. I like cookies."

Characteristics. This 50-item subtest taps a student's understanding of word meaning. The examiner dictates a statement, and the student must decide if it is true or not. An example is "All trees are oaks." Guessing may affect results of this subtest.

Word Ordering. This 20-item subtest assesses the ability to use correct syntax in speech. The student's task is to reorder words dictated by the examiner to form a correct and complete sentence. An example is "hard, rained, it." The number of words dictated varies from three to seven.

Generals. The ability to use correct semantics in speech is assessed on 25 items. The examiner dictates three words, and the student must indicate how the words are alike. An example is "hot, cold, warm."

Grammatic Completion. The 40 items on this subtest tap a student's understanding of correct syntax. The examiner dictates sentences, and the student's task is to indicate whether each sentence is correct or not. Various types of errors are involved, such as noun-verb agreement, plurals, and adverbs. Guessing may be a factor on this subtest.

Technical Adequacy

Standardization. There were 871 students in the sample. The demographic characteristics favorably compare to data in the 1980 *Statistical Abstracts of the United States* in terms of sex, urban-rural residence, geographic distribution, and occupation of parents. There was a similarity on the variable of race, but black students were somewhat underrepresented (i.e., 6% instead of 12%).

Reliability. Test-retest reliability data are provided only for fifth and sixth graders with a one-week interval. Correlations for subtests ranged from .83 to .92 and for composites from .94 to .96.

For internal consistency, the correlations for the subtests ranged from .70 to .98 and for composites from .91 to .98.

Standard errors of measurement are provided for all subtests and composites by age level.

Validity. Each item was subjected to analysis in terms of item difficulty and discriminating power and found to be acceptable. Further, in the development of the TOLD–I, 50 professionals evaluated the subtests in terms of whether they measured semantics, syntax, listening, and speaking. The subtests were rated as being consistent with the language model on which the test was built.

For criterion-related validity, the TOLD–I was compared to the *Test of Adolescent Language.* Subtest correlations ranged from .35 to .74; composite correlations ranged from .35 to .83.

For construct validity, the mean scores were found to increase with age. Intercorrelations of subtests ranged from .30 to .57. The TOLD–I subtests were found to discriminate between a group of LD students and a matched control group.

Conclusions. Fortunately, the entire TOLD–I does not require vision. Though black students were underrepresented, the other demographic characteristics of the sample correspond closely to census data.

Reliability data are good, but test-retest data by age level are needed.

The validity of the TOLD–I appears to be sound.

This test could be used to provide comprehensive information on language skills for students with little or no vision. No adaptations are needed. Guessing may result in inflated scores on some subtests.

Test of Language Development-Primary

(See critique in Chapter 4.)

Vineland Adaptive Behavior Scales–Expanded Form

Authors: Sara S. Sparrow, David A. Balla, and
Domenic V. Cicchetti

Publisher: American Guidance Service
Publishers Building
Circle Pines, MN 55014-1796

Copyright: 1984

General Description. The *Vineland Adaptive Behavior Scales* are made up of three tests: the Interview Edition, Survey Form; the Interview Edition, Expanded Form; and the Classroom Edition. The Scales were designed to provide norm-referenced scores and detailed information for planning individual programs. The Expanded Form will be reviewed because it provides more extensive information, can be used for children from birth to 18 years, and provides a better sample of behavior than the Survey Form. The Classroom Edition is designed only for students from 3 years to 12 years, 11 months of age. The scales are designed to measure "... the performance of the daily activities required for personal and social sufficiency" (p. 6).

The Expanded Form is made up of six domains: Communication, Daily Living Skills, Socialization, Motor Skills, and Maladaptive Behavior. These can be broken down into subdomains and combined to obtain an Adaptive Behavior Composite.

Results for the domains and the Adaptive Behavior Composite are expressed as standard scores (mean = 100, standard deviation = 15), Percentile ranks, stanines, adaptive levels (e.g., *high, moderately high*), and age equivalents. Adaptive levels and age equivalents may be determined for the subdomains.

There are also supplementary norms for different groups of handicapped individuals. Results for these norms can be expressed as percentile ranks for domains and the Adaptive Behavior Composite. Adaptive levels can be determined for domains, the Composite, and subdomains.

Administration time for the Expanded Form is from 60 to 90 minutes. Information is obtained by interviewing the parent or caregiver. Items are scored 2 (yes, usually), 1 (sometimes or partially), 0 (no, never), N (no opportunity) and DK (don't know).

Materials needed for this form are an item booklet, a summary and profile booklet, a manual, and a program planning report.

Description of Domains

Communication. This domain contains 133 items: 23 for receptive skills, 76 for expressive skills, and 34 for written skills. The subdomains for receptive and expressive skills could be used on students with little or no vision. The Written Subdomain contains items that students with little or no vision would not be able to perform unless the items were adapted (e.g., "copies at least 5 letters of the alphabet from a model," "addresses envelopes completely"). It would not be possible to adapt some of these items. An examiner could leave this domain out of the assessment and use results only from the other two subdomains, or indicate that the score obtained should be interpreted considering the fact that many of the items required vision.

Daily Living Skills. There are 201 items for this domain. The Personal Subdomain contains 90 items, the Domestic Subdomain 45 items, and the Community Domain 66 items. Most of the Personal items could be used with visually impaired and blind students. Examples are "Eats solid food" and "Covers mouth and nose when coughing and sneezing." Some of the skills (e.g., use of fasteners and caring for hair) may develop later for visually impaired and blind children than sighted children. This should be considered when interpreting scores. One item that would need to be adapted or not administered is "Uses oral thermometer without assistance." Many items on the Domestic Subdomain must be adapted and some may not be appropriate for students with little or no vision. Examples are "Uses basic tools" and "Uses household cleaning products appropriately and correctly." (This latter item requires that the student be able to read the instructions on products.) This applies to the Community Domain also. Examples of inappropriate items for students who have little or no useful vision are "Obeys traffic lights and Walk and Don't Walk signs" and "Discriminates between bills of different denominations."

Socialization. There are 134 items on this domain: 50 for Interpersonal Relationships, 48 for Play and Leisure Time, and 36 for Coping Skills. Numerous items at the lower level of Interpersonal Relationships require vision (e.g., "Follows with eyes a person moving at cribside or bedside"). Upper level items are more appropriate (e.g., "Converses with others on topics of mutual interest"). For Play and Leisure Time, most items can be used with children with little or no vision, though several items may require adaptive materials. Examples of items that require special materials are the items on card or board games. Items for Coping Skills do not require vision.

Motor Skills. Seventy-three items make up this domain: 42 are for Gross Motor and 31 for Fine Motor. Many of the early skills on the Gross Motor subdomain are those likely to be delayed in developing for children with little or no vision (e.g., sitting and walking). For the Fine Motor domain, items completing puzzles, drawing, and some items for using scissors require vision.

Maladaptive Behavior. This domain is appropriate for use only with students who are 5 years of age or older. There are two parts to the domain; Part 1 describes minor maladaptive behaviors, and Part 2 is for more serious problem behaviors. Part 1 has 21 items. Examples of the behaviors measured are, "Is overly active" and "Teases or bullies." For Part 2, only the supplementary norm groups can be used for comparison. Items are rated for frequency and intensity. Examples of the more serious behaviors are, "Uses bizarre speech" and "Displays behaviors that are self-injurious."

Technical Adequacy

Standardization. Only the Survey Form of the Scales was standardized. Norms for the Expanded Form were developed based on data from the standardization of the Survey using the Rasch-Wright item calibration estimates (an item-sampling procedure). The Survey Form and Maladaptive Behavior Domain were standardized on 3,000 individuals, with 200 subjects per age level (birth to 18 years). There were 1,500 females in the sample. The demographic characteristics of the sample closely resembled the 1980 census data in terms of geographic distribution, educational attainment of parents, race or ethnic group, and community size. The sample also corresponded to the census data in terms of educational placement (e.g., regular classroom, classroom for mentally retarded). The "other" category for educational placement included visually handicapped children (as well as deaf, orthopedically impaired, etc.). The "other" category makes up .7% of the U.S. population; .4% of the *Vineland* sample (i.e., 12 children) fit the "other" category. Twelve children is obviously an insufficient number to adequately represent this heterogenous subgroup of children.

Supplementary norms were developed for several handicapping conditions. Included as one of these groups were 200 visually handicapped children, 6 through 12-11 years of age, attending residential facilities. These norms are not likely to be representative of most visually impaired and blind students today, because most of these students attend public schools rather than residential facilities.

Reliability. Test-retest reliability data are presented for the Survey Form for 484 subjects from 6 through 18-11 years of age. A 2- to 4-week retest interval was employed. Correlation coefficients across the domains ranged from .80 to .98. For the Maladaptive Behavior section (*n* = 340, ages 5-0 to 8-11), correlations ranged from .84 to .89.

Internal consistency correlation coefficients for the Expanded Form ranged from .83 to .97 for the domains, from .94 to .99 for the Adaptive Behavior Composite, and from .77 to .88 for the Maladaptive Behavior (Part 1). Internal Consistency correlations for Supplementary Norms ranged from .95 to .99 for the domains. Correlations for the Composite were all .99. Maladaptive Behavior correlations ranged from .76 to .90 (Part 1) and from .85 to .92 (Parts 1 and 2).

Interrater reliability was assessed for the Survey and ranged from .96 to .99 across the domains. For Part 1 of the Maladaptive Behavior Domain a coefficient of .74 was obtained.

Validity. In terms of content validity, the items were developed from a review of other adaptive behavior measures and the child development literature. These items were field tested and then subjected to a tryout on a national basis.

For concurrent validity, the test was compared to the original *Vineland* with a correlation of .55. The test was also compared to *Adaptive Behavior Inventory for Children* (ABIC) and correlated .58 (*n* = 9), and the *AAMD Adaptive Behavior Scale* and correlated .40 to .70 across domains. The *Vineland Scale* was examined in terms of its relationship to the *Kaufman–ABC*, and correlations ranged from .07 to .52. Correlation ranges with the PPVT–R were .12 to .37 for the domains. The relationship of *Vineland Scale* (Survey) results for the supplementary norms and IQ test results were assessed, and the following correlation ranges were obtained for visually handicapped children in residential facilities: WISC–R (*n* = 23), .48 to .77; *Hayes-Binet* (*n* = 21), .73 to .84; and *Perkins-Binet* (*n* = 23), .45 to .83.

In terms of construct validity, mean scores tend to increase with age. Factor analyses seem to support the structure of the test.

It should be noted that investigation of the mean standard scores showed that the visually handicapped group had the largest deficits in adaptive behavior in all areas, compared to hearing impaired and emotionally impaired students. This is probably due to the fact that many items require vision and hence are inappropriate for this group of students.

Conclusions. The standardization, reliability, and validity data for the *Vineland* are impressive. However, when used with visually impaired and blind students, two problems exist. Many items require vision. This is more of a problem for some domains than others. Thus, these students will be penalized on these items. If the supplementary norms for visually handicapped are used, these are representative only of the performance of students in residential programs. Whether performance of public school students differs remains to be investigated, but similar performance cannot be assumed.

Any test that uses an interview format can yield results that may not accurately characterize a student's performance. The accuracy is largely a function of the objectivity and reliability of the informant. Questionable information is best followed-up by direct observation of the student's performance in the natural environment.

This version of the *Vineland* is a major improvement over the prior version. It could provide useful information for program planning, and may or may not yield valid scores for blind and visually impaired students. Whether scores are valid depends on the informant, the number of items that cannot be scored because of the visual problem, and the type of educational program the student attends.

Wechsler Adult Intelligence Scale–Revised

Author: David Wechsler

Publisher: The Psychological Corporation
555 Academic Court
San Antonio, TX 78204

Copyright: 1981

General Description. The *Wechsler Adult Intelligence Scale–Revised* (WAIS–R) was designed for adults who are from 16 years through 74 years, 11 months of age.

The WAIS–R is made up of a Verbal Scale and a Performance Scale. Because the Performance Scale requires vision, only the Verbal Scale will be reviewed. The Verbal Scale contains six subtests: Information, Digit Span, Vocabulary, Arithmetic, Comprehension, and Similarities.

Results are in terms of scaled scores for subtests and quotients for the Verbal and Performance Scales and for the total score.

Administration time is 60 to 90 minutes for Full Scale Score. Approximately half this time would be needed to give only the Verbal Scale.

Materials for the Verbal Scale consist of a manual, record book, and seven blocks. A list of words in braille or large print for the Vocabulary subtest may be helpful, but is not required.

Description of Subtests

Information. There are 29 questions on this subtest for which the examiner asks a question and for which the student is to verbally respond. Examples are "What is the shape of a ball?" and "On what continent is the Sahara Desert?"

Digit Span. This subtest contains 14 items. For the first 7 items, the examiner reads a string of 3 to 9 digits and the student is to repeat them. For the other 7 items, the examiner gives a string of digits and the student must repeat them backwards.

Vocabulary. There are 35 items on this subtest. The examiner presents a copy of the word list to the student, reads each word and points to it, and the student is asked to tell what each word means. A braille or large print list of the words would be helpful for visually impaired and blind students. Examples of words are "penny" and "tirade."

Arithmetic. For this subtest, 14 arithmetic problems are orally presented and the student is asked for a verbal response. Only the first item requires blocks. For this item, seven blocks are placed on the table and the student is to answer the question, "How many blocks are there altogether?" A student with little or no vision would have to count the blocks by touch.

Comprehension. There are 16 items where the examiner asks questions such as "Why are child labor laws needed?"

Similarities. Fourteen items require the student to indicate how two things are alike. Examples include "egg–seed" and "fly–tree."

Technical Adequacy

Standardization. The 1970 census data were used to select the sample. There were from 160 to 300 subjects per age level and there were equal numbers of males and females. Race by geographic region characteristics closely approximate the census data. The proportion of white and nonwhite subjects for each occupational category is also very similar to census data, as is the educational level of the sample. Urban-rural residence is reasonably close to that of the U.S. population.

Reliability. The WAIS–R is appropriate for school-age students from 16 through 25 years of age. However, there are no test-retest data for these ages. For an age group of 25 to 34 year old subjects, the correlations for the Verbal Scale (2–7 week retest interval) ranged from .79 to .93. The Verbal Scale total correlation was .94. Test-retest data are needed for the various age levels of the test.

Internal consistency correlations for the Verbal Scale for age levels 16-17 and 18-19 range from .70 to .96. Verbal Scale total correlations were .95 and .96, respectively.

Standard errors of measurement are given by age level for subtests, both scales, and the Full Scale IQ score.

Validity. In terms of content validity, tests were selected based on ratings of experienced clinicians, correlations with other tests of intelligence, and studies of several groups with known levels of intellectual performance. Many studies have been carried out to show that persons with lower levels of education do less well on the WAIS–R than those with a more extensive educational background. Research has shown that results of this test correlate with school performance.

Results of factor analytic studies tend to support the structure of the test.

Many studies have examined the relationship of the WAIS and WAIS–R to other tests of intelligence. One study reported in the manual showed a correlation of .85 with the WAIS–R and Binet for 52 male prisoners.

Conclusions. Standardization is excellent in terms of being representative and having a sufficient number of subjects per level.

Reliability data are also good, except that test-retest data are needed by age level.

The validity data seem to be adequate.

The Verbal Scale requires modification on only one item for students with little or no vision. This part of the test is likely to provide a valid normed score for comparing the performance of a student with little or no vision with that of sighted students. However, because of the lack of sufficient test-retest data, information from other measures would also be necessary.

Wechsler Intelligence Scale for Children–Revised

Author: David Wechsler

Publisher: The Psychological Corporation
            555 Academic Court
            San Antonio, TX 78204

Copyright: 1974

General Description. The *Wechsler Intelligence Scale for Children–Revised* (WISC–R) was designed for children from 6½ through 16½ years old.

The test consists of 10 subtests, five of which make up the Verbal Scale and five the Performance Scale. There is also one supplementary subtest for each scale. Only the Verbal Scale does not require vision, hence this is the only scale that will be reviewed. This Scale includes the following subtests: Information, Similarities, Arithmetic, Vocabulary, Comprehension, and Digit Span (supplementary). Digit Span can be used as an additional test or can be substituted for a regularly-administered subtest that for some reason could not be properly administered. See a discussion of the effects of this substitution under Cognitive Development in this chapter.

Results are in terms of scaled scores for subtests and quotients for the Verbal and Performance Scales and for the Full Scale score.

Administration time is about 50 to 75 minutes for the full scale and approximately half this time for only the Verbal Scale.

Materials for the Verbal Scale consist of a manual and a record form. No adaptations are presented for visually impaired or blind students. However, if the Verbal Scale is used with a student who has little or no vision, and if the student is less than 8 years old or is suspected of being mentally impaired, it will be necessary to prepare a raised-figure card for items 1 through 4 on the Arithmetic subtest. These items require counting figures on the card.

Description of the Subtests

Information. This subtest consists of 30 items where the examiner asks the student questions that require a verbal response. Examples are "What does the stomach do?" and "Who was Charles Darwin?"

Similarities. There are 17 possible items on this subtest. The student is asked to tell how two things, such as a piano and a guitar, are alike.

Arithmetic. Eighteen items make up this subtest. The first four require that the student use a card with pictures of 12 trees on it. The student is asked to count various quantities of trees using the card. Raised figures would be necessary for students with little or no vision. The remaining 14 arithmetic problems can be verbally presented, and the student is asked to verbally respond.

Vocabulary. On this 32-item subtest the student is asked to define words such as "brave" and "affliction."

Comprehension. There are 17 items on this subtest. Students must verbally answer questions presented by the examiner. An example is "Why are criminals locked up?"

Digit Span. This supplementary subtest provides an estimate of the student's ability to remember material she or he hears. This can be useful information when planning classroom programs for students with little or no vision who must rely heavily on auditory input for learning. On this subtest, there are 7 items where the student repeats from 3 to 9 digits given by the examiner. There are also 7 items with 3 to 9 digits for which the student is asked to repeat the string of digits backwards.

Technical Adequacy

Standardization. The sample for the WISC–R was made up of 100 girls and 100 boys per age level, making a total of 2,200 subjects. The demographic data for the sample closely correspond to the 1970 census data in terms of geographic distribution, race (white and nonwhite), occupation of head of household, and urban-rural residence. Further, the racial make-up of the subjects from each geographic region closely corresponds to the census data.

Reliability. Test-retest data are presented for 303 children whose demographic characteristics were similar to the census data for race, sex and occupation of head of household. The children were from the four regions of the country and from both urban and rural areas. A one-month retest interval was employed. Data are given only for three age groupings. Correlations for the Verbal Scale for ages 6½ to 7½ ranged from .70 to .84 (Verbal IQ .90), for ages 10½ to 11½ ranged from .73 to .86 (Verbal IQ .95), and for ages 14½ to 15½ ranged from .78 to .92 (Verbal IQ .94). The Verbal IQ correlations are sufficiently high to use in making eligibility decisions, but test-retest data are needed on the WISC–R for each age level.

Internal consistency data on Verbal subtests ranged from .67 to .92. Verbal IQ correlations ranged from .91 to .96.

Standard errors of measurement are given for each subtest, both scales, and the total score. These are presented by age level.

Validity. The average intercorrelation of the subtests on the Verbal Scale ranged from .26 to .69. Average intercorrelations of the Verbal IQ and the Verbal subtests ranged from .45 to .78.

In terms of concurrent validity, the WISC–R has been compared with many other tests. In the manual, correlations are reported with the *Wechsler Preschool and Primary Scale of Intelligence* (WPPSI), the *Wechsler Adult Intelligence Scale* (WAIS), and the *Stanford-Binet*. Correlations of the Verbal subtests for the WISC–R and WPPSI ranged from .39 to .70 (Verbal IQ .80). With the WAIS, the Verbal Scale subtest correlations ranged from .73 to .91 (Verbal IQ .96). Correlations of WISC–R Verbal subtests and the Binet for four age levels ranged from .11 to .75. Verbal IQ and Binet IQ correlations ranged from .64 to .77.

Conclusions. Standardization, reliability and validity are good for the WISC–R. More test-retest data are needed by age level.

The Verbal Scale could be used to compare children with little or no vision to sighted students. Minimal modifications are needed on the Arithmetic subtest. The results would need to be supplemented with data from other tests because of limited reliability and the fact that some verbal skills require more time to develop for these children. This is particularly a concern for young children.

Wechsler Preschool and Primary Scale of Intelligence

(See review in Chapter 4.)

Wide Range Achievement Test

Authors: Sarah Jastak and Gary Wilkinson

Publisher: Jastak Associates, Inc.
            1526 Gilpin Avenue
            Wilmington, DE 19806

Braille   American Printing House for the Blind
and large   1839 Frankfort Ave.
print   P.O. Box 6085
versions: Louisville, KY 40296

Copyright: 1965, 1976, 1978, 1984

General Description.   The *Wide Range Achievement Test* (WRAT) is made up of two levels: one for children from 5 to 11-11 years of age and the other for students from 12 years of age to adult. Vision is required for this test, but braille and large print transcriptions are available from the American Printing House for the Blind.

The WRAT is composed of three subtests: Spelling, Arithmetic, and Reading. Both levels have the same subtests.

Scores can be interpreted in terms of standard scores, percentiles, and grade ratings. However, an addendum to the manual states that the test was normed on age, not grade levels. Consequently, the grade ratings should not be used as normed scores.

The administration time is from 20 to 30 minutes, but more time will be required for the transcribed versions.

The only materials needed are a manual and record book.

Description of Subtests

Spelling. This subtest involves copying 18 marks, writing the student's name, and writing 46 words dictated by the examiner. Copying marks is not a spelling skill. It is possible for a child in first grade (from 6-0 to 6-5 years of age) to score within the average range and not be able to spell a word on the test.

Arithmetic. This subtest taps various skills: counting, reading number symbols, solving oral problems, and performing written computations (addition, subtraction, multiplication, division, percents, decimals, Roman numerals, square roots, and fractions).

Reading. This subtest requires matching and naming letters and pronouncing isolated words. Matching letters of the alphabet is not a reading skill. Word recognition is only one of the many skills involved in reading. Only 15 words on Level I and 5 on Level II are high frequency words (Lesiak & Bradley-Johnson, 1983). Hence, this subtest taps only a very limited sample of reading behavior. It is also possible for a first grader (age 6-0 to 6-5) to score within the average range (i.e., 85 + standard score), but not be able to read a word on the test.

Technical Adequacy

Standardization. In the sample for the WRAT there were 5,600 subjects. Age groups are in half year intervals with 200 subjects per level. Data correspond closely to 1982 *Rand McNally Atlas* data for geographic distribution, sex, race, and metropolitan/ nonmetropolitan residence. No data are given for socioeconomic level.

Reliability. Test-retest correlations for Level I were .96 for Reading, .97 for Spelling, and .94 for Arithmetic. For Level II correlations were .90 for Reading, .89 for Spelling, and .79 for Arithmetic. Length of the retest interval was not given.

Split-half reliability coefficients for Levels I and II were in the .90's.
Standard errors of measurement are given.

Validity. Scores tend to increase with age.

Validity data are given for only the 1946 and 1965 editions. No other validity data are presented for the current version.

Concerns about the content validity were noted under the description of the subtests.

Conclusions. The content of the Reading and Spelling subtests is the most serious problem for the WRAT. Further, data on socioeconomic status of the standardization sample are needed, as are test-retest data by age level with a specified interval. There are too few items to use the information for planning educational programs. The poor content validity makes the WRAT technically inadequate for use in eligibility decisions for visually impaired, blind, or sighted students.

Criterion-Referenced Tests and Informal Measures

For a discussion of the use of criterion-referenced tests and informal measures, see Chapter 4. Instruments were selected for review if (a) they

TABLE 6
Criterion Referenced Tests and Informal Measures for Blind and Visually Impaired Students

	Areas Assessed
Braille Unit Recognition Battery (for students who have had training in braille)	Knowledge of braille
Diagnostic Inventory of Early Development (Birth to 7 years)	Motor, language, self help, readiness, reading, and arithmetic
Dolch Word List (6 to 9 years)	Knowledge of sight words
Informal Assessment of Developmental Skills for Visually Handicapped Students (Birth through school age)	Visual functioning, unique academic needs (e.g., Optacon, typewriter, braillewriter), orientation and mobility, vocational skills, and behavior
Oregon Project for Visually Impaired and Blind Infants and Preschoolers (Birth to age 6)	Cognitive, language, self-help, socialization, fine motor, and gross motor

had been published within the past 15 years (so that the content was appropriate) and (b) did not require vision for most of the items.

Many criterion-referenced tests have been published for sighted school-age students. Though these tests could be adapted for students with little or no vision, extensive adaptations would be required, sometimes for nearly the entire test. The most comprehensive of these tests are the *Brigance Diagnostic Comprehensive Inventory of Basic Skills* (Brigance, 1983) for elementary and middle schools, and the *Brigance Diagnostic Inventory of Essential Skills* (Brigance, 1981) for use in secondary schools. Additional advantages of these tests over most other criterion-referenced tests is that skills are appropriately tested and each skill is tested two to four times (Bradley-Johnson & Lesiak, 1981; Lesiak & Bradley-Johnson, 1983). See Table 6 for a list of tests evaluated in this section and areas assessed by each.

The material that follows consists of detailed reviews for criterion-referenced tests and informal measures. When data on the technical adequacy of these instruments were provided, these data were evaluated in the reviews. Descriptions of the content of the tests, administration procedures, and the materials are included. Adaptations are necessary for two of the measures; the remaining three instruments were designed specifically for visually impaired and blind students.

Braille Unit Recognition Battery: Diagnostic Test of Grade 2 Literary Braille

Authors: Hilda Caton, Bill Duckworth, and Earl Rankin

Publisher: American Printing House for the Blind
             P.O. Box 6085
             Louisville, KY 40206-0085

Copyright: 1985

General Description. This battery is designed primarily for students in grades 3 through 12, but can be used with younger children and older adults. The main purpose of the battery is to assess students' abilities to recognize and identify the different braille units, and from this information to determine which units require additional instruction. The battery can also be used to determine whether a student's overall ability to read braille reaches a level considered to be indicative of a competent braille reader.

Item selection and organization of the battery were based on *Patterns: The Primary Braille Reading Program* (Caton, Pester, & Bradley, 1980), which was designed to teach braille. Thus, the three sections of the battery are: Letters, Grams, and Modulations.

Administration of the battery can be done individually or in groups and about one hour is required. However, there are no time limits.

Materials consist of the test manual, a booklet for the student, a record form for reporting scores, and a checklist used to assess physical aspects of braille reading, such as posture and hand position.

Items are orally presented by the examiner, and students mark their answers in the test booklet using a pencil or crayon. There are either four or five alternatives for each item, from which a student selects his or her answer. Practice in marking answers is given prior to the administration of the test items.

This battery should be administered by a psychologist or teacher who is familiar with working with visually impaired and blind students. This includes having knowledge of the educational needs of these students and thorough knowledge of grade 2 literary braille.

Description and Evaluation of Sections

Letters. Two tests make up this section: Alphabetic Letters and Nonalphabetic Letters (numbers). The first test consists of recognizing each of the 26 letters of the alphabet. The second test requires recognition of the one-digit numbers 0 through 9, two-digit numbers (10 items), and three-digit numbers (10 items).

Grams. There are three tests for this section: Phonograms, Morphograms, and Letter Words and Wordlets. The Phonogram Test is made up of 50 one-shape (e.g., *ch, gh*) and multishape (e.g., *ity, less*) phonograms. A phonogram is a unit of braille written in print with more than one alphabetic symbol. The Morphogram Test taps knowledge of the elements of braille that have the value of a word element; these include prefixes, suffixes and inflectional endings. There are 27 items on this test (e.g., "con" and "ed"). The Letter Words and Wordlets Test has two parts. Letter words are words that also have letter values, and there are 23 such items (e.g., "very", "can"). Wordlets involve one or more shapes with a word value, but no letter value. The 129 wordlets tested are divided into four subtests: one-shape, two-shape, three-shape, and four- and five-shape wordlets.

Modulations. This section taps recognition of braille units for punctuation, register, and some additional nonalphabetic letters not previously tested. There are 30 items on this section. Punctuation items include those that look back, such as a period or question mark; those that enclose material, such as quotation marks or parentheses; and those that link material, such as a dash or hyphen. Register items include a variety of units, such as those for italics or capitals. Nonalphabetic letters assessed in this section are braille units, such as the decimal point and apostrophe.

Braille Mechanics. This part of the battery can be completed before or after administration of the battery. The checklist has 16 items, and each item has three to five alternatives to choose from to describe a student's behavior when reading braille. Items describe a variety of behaviors, such as position of fingers, amount of pressure on fingertips, use of remaining vision, and use of either hand or both hands. These behaviors are helpful to note because correction of inappropriate behaviors could aid the student in reading braille more accurately and efficiently.

Technical Adequacy

Field Testing. An initial pool of 945 items was generated, consisting of three items for every unit of braille in each of the categories. This pool of items was field tested in three residential schools with 67 students (grades 3 through 12), who had at least one year of instruction in reading braille, and who had no impairments in addition to blindness. An experimental version of the battery with 315 items was developed after faulty items were eliminated, and items that were likely to result in a large number of correct responses were selected. This version was again field tested with 150 students (grades 3 through 12) from residential and day school programs. These students also had had at least one year of instruction in reading braille and had no impairments besides blindness. Item analysis indicated that these items were satisfactory and that nearly all students had 80% or more of the items correct.

Based on this information, and input from six braille consultants, the mastery level was set at 90%. This criterion was considered minimum for proficient braille reading.

Validity. Items were selected based on a review of existing tests and using the braille terms developed for teaching braille reading (Caton et al., 1980). All units for grade 2 literary braille were included, except for diacritical marks and units of braille used in foreign languages.

To avoid confusion that occurs with other tests, the format of this battery requires that students read and mark only single units of braille and that the examiner present only single units of braille. Finally, the categories of braille used do not group together braille units that are easily confused. Because of this, it is easier to determine the specific skills a student has learned for reading braille and those that require additional work.

The difficulty level of the items was kept low so that the battery could be used to identify students whose basic braille skills are so poor that special assistance is necessary.

Reliability. The Subkoviak Group Coefficient of Agreement suggests that students who met the criterion and those who did not would fall into similar categories if they were to retake the battery. Standard errors of measurement are provided for each part of the battery. Pearson correlations suggest that the various parts of the battery are moderately related. Because a multiple-choice format is used, some results could be affected by guessing, resulting in an overestimate of a student's ability .

Conclusions.   Results of this battery could be very useful for determining which units of braille need to be taught to students who are not proficient in reading and which do not need to be taught. It is important to keep in mind that the battery should be administered only by someone who thoroughly understands grade 2 literary braille and the needs of visually impaired and blind students. If for some reason an examiner suspects that results may be inflated due to guessing, it would be relatively easy to construct additional items to test further for the skills in question, using the same format. The format of this battery was carefully thought out, and the information from the tests and checklist of behaviors is comprehensive. This criterion-referenced test is an important contribution to assessment of visually impaired and blind students.

Diagnostic Inventory of Early Development

(The critique for this inventory is presented in Chapter 4.)

Figure 8. Dolch word list. (Courtesy the American Printing House for the Blind.)

Dolch Word List

Author:	Edward Dolch

Publisher: Braille and large print versions available from the
American Printing House for the Blind, Inc.
1839 Frankford Ave.
P.O. Box 6085
Louisville, KY 40206-0085

Copyright: 1955

General Description. This word list is most appropriate for students in the early grades, about ages 6 to 9. The words were selected based on words commonly taught in basal series for these grades.

The materials consist of 220 cards, each with one word printed in braille and in large type. Cards are 3½ × 2 inches in size. The materials for this list are displayed in Figure 8.

Though there have been many changes in basal series since the publication of this list, most writers agree that words on the list make up about 50% of the vocabulary in elementary grade materials, that many words are taught consistently from one series to the next, and that most words are taught in grades one and two (Lesiak & Bradley-Johnson, 1983). Hence, this list was included for review.

To administer the list, cards are presented one at a time to a student. The student's task is to tell the examiner what each word is.

Conclusions.   The Dolch list in braille or large print would provide useful information on a student's word recognition skills. However, it would be worthwhile to supplement this list with words from the Fry (1980) list of instant words. Words on the Fry list frequently occur in materials a person might read throughout a lifetime. The list is based on a frequency count of more than five million running words that appeared in 500 word samples, from 1,045 books in twelve subject areas, fiction and nonfiction books, and magazines (Carroll, Davies, & Richman, 1971). The first 10 words make up 24% of words found in written material, the first 100 make up 50%, and the 300 words on the list account for 65% of the words in written material. It is obvious that these words are critical for reading. Most are mastered by third grade. The Dolch list is based on those commonly *taught*, but the Fry list contains those that are frequently *encountered* in reading. The Fry list is more comprehensive.

In order to use the Fry words that do not appear on the Dolch list, the additional words would have to be printed on cards in braille or large print.

Informal Assessment of Developmental Skills For Visually Handicapped Students (School-Age Section).

Authors: Rose-Marie Swallow, Sally Mangold, and Philip Mangold

Publisher: American Foundation for the Blind
15 W. 16th St.
New York, NY 10011

Copyright: 1978

General Description.   This is a series of checklists designed to help assess the special needs of students with little or no vision in the classroom. The checklists were prepared by teachers of visually handicapped students.

Some of the checklists are sequential and can aid in setting teaching objectives, others involve more functional skills (e.g., orientation and mobility), and some are both.

The authors give permission to duplicate the checklists for "educational use with visually handicapped children" (p. 2).

Description of Checklists. The checklists are grouped in terms of the areas assessed.

Visual Functioning. Two checklists are included for this area. One is used to describe a student's functional vision both indoors and outside and the optimal conditions for sight. Examples of items include conditions needed for optimal viewing of audiovisual materials, classroom modifications, and whether the student can see traffic lights during the day and at night. This checklist is quite lengthy and involves observation of the student in numerous settings (e.g., classroom, auditorium, a building with escalators, and outdoors). The other checklist primarily involves reading print. It includes information on eye condition, visual aids, type of print, and reading skills (e.g., reading behaviors, interests, and word attack skills). The reading behaviors are particularly helpful for these students (e.g., "Tilts head and/or book" and "Jumps lines on return sweep"). However, reading skills would be more comprehensively assessed by the *Brigance* tests.

Unique Academic Needs. Twelve checklists are presented to tap communication skills needed for academic success. Two checklists assess braille reading skills, two tap listening abilities, two involve a task analysis of use of the Optacon, one taps skills needed to use a braillewriter, one assesses abilities required for use of a slate and stylus, one taps script writing for blind students, one is to assess script writing for low vision students, and the last two assess typing skills. The production checklists (i.e., those involving the braillewriter, slate and stylus, script writing, and typing skills) are particularly helpful. However, on the typing skills checklists it is not clear on all items what is being tested, and a number of skills listed are not critical (e.g., "Elbow close to side of body" and "Machine Parts-Erasure Table"). The checklists in this section are based on detailed analyses of these tasks and could provide useful, specific information for planning educational programs. Consideration of listening skills is very important for visually impaired and blind students because so much information must be obtained via this modality. The two listening abilities checklists highlight critical skills.

Orientation and Mobility. As noted by the authors, these checklists are not designed for the O & M instructor nor the adaptive physical education specialist. Rather, they are more general and aimed at tapping skills that the classroom teacher can work on in the classroom that are related to orientation and mobility. For school districts that do not have the services of an O & M instructor, these scales will be helpful so that at least some basic orientation and mobility skills can be addressed. Five checklists are presented. One checklist can be used to test spatial reasoning and fine-motor control in terms of use of blocks, puzzles, paper and crayons, bead stringing, cutting, tying, and pouring. A second checklist is to tap gross motor skills including balance and coordination, strength, agility, rhythm, and endurance. The third checklist is for measuring knowledge of body parts, movements, laterality, and directionality. A fourth checklist can be used to tap left-right discrimination and spatial orientation. The last checklist has 59 tasks including body concepts, relational concepts, and movement around objects. It is helpful, but not necessary, to videotape when testing skills on this last checklist.

Vocational Skills. Two checklists are available for this area. One assesses adaptive behaviors such as survival skills (e.g., "Locates public rest-rooms," "Mails a letter," and "Knows what to do if lost"), use of the telephone, and organizational skills. Numerous skills are included that are especially important for visually impaired and blind students and that are not included on other scales. Because some items are general (e.g., "Cares for skin" and "Shows up for appointments"), subjective judgment is involved in scoring. The second checklist can be used to tap a variety of prevocational skills, such as personal development (e.g., "Dresses appropriately" and "Poise and emotional control"), daily living skills, and basic manipulative skills.

Behavioral Rating Scale. This is a detailed checklist containing items relevant to classroom success. A wide range of behaviors is included, such as skills in organization, listening, language, self-discipline, and attention.

Technical Adequacy. No data are given on field testing, reliability, or validity. Hence, the results must be interpreted in light of the informal nature of the checklists.

Conclusions. These checklists can provide detailed information which would be very helpful for planning instructional programs for visually impaired and blind students. The checklists do in fact consider many unique needs of these students. Given the subjective and general nature of the checklists for vocational skills and behavior, results must be cautiously interpreted. The checklists are a much-needed contribution to the field and are important to consider in the assessment of any school-aged student with little or no vision.

Oregon Project for Visually Impaired and Blind Infants and Preschoolers

(The review for this inventory appears in Chapter 4.)

References

Alessi, G., & Kaye, J. H. (1983). *Behavior assessment for school psychologists.* Stratford, CT: NASP Publications Office.

American Foundation for the Blind. (Undated). *Facts About Blindness.* New York.

Anderson, D. W., & Olson, M. R. (1981). Word meaning among congenitally blind children. *Journal of Visual Impairment and Blindness, 75,* 165–168.

Ashman, S. (1982). *An introduction to psychological assessment of visually impaired children.* Indianapolis: Indiana State School for the Blind.

Bauman, M. K. (1973). Psychological and educational assessment. In B. Lowenfeld (Ed.), *The visually handicapped child in school.* New York: John Day.

Bayley, N. (1969). *Bayley Scales of Infant Development.* San Antonio: The Psychological Corporation.

Boehm, A. (1971). *Boehm Test of Basic Concepts.* San Antonio: The Psychological Corporation.

Bradley-Johnson, S. (in press). *Cognitive Abilities Relevant to Education.* Austin, TX: PRO-ED.

Bradley-Johnson, S., & Lesiak, J. (1981). *Assessment of written expression. A critique of procedures and instruments.* Brandon, VT: Clinical Psychology Publishing Company.

Brigance, A. (1983). *Brigance Diagnostic Comprehensive Inventory of Basic Skills.* North Billerica, MA: Curriculum Associates.

Brigance, A. (1981). *Brigance Diagnostic Inventory of Essential Skills.* North Billerica, MA: Curriculum Associates.

Brigance, A. (1978). *Diagnostic Inventory of Early Development.* North Billerica, MA: Curriculum Associates.

Brown, D., Simmons, V., & Methvin, J. (1979). *The Oregon Project for Visually Impaired and Blind Preschool Children.* Medford, OR: Jackson County Education Service District.

Carroll, J., Davies, P., & Richman, B. (1971). *The American Heritage word frequency book.* Boston: Houghton-Mifflin.

Carrow, E. (1974). *Carrow Elicited Language Inventory.* Allen, TX: DLM/Teaching Resources.

Caton, H., Duckworth, B., & Rankin, E. (1985). *Braille Unit Recognition Battery.* Louisville, KY: American Printing House for the Blind.

Caton, H., Pester, H., & Bradley, E. J. (1980). *Patterns: The primary braille reading program.* Louisville, KY: American Printing House for the Blind.

Caton, H. R. (1976). *Tactile Test of Basic Concepts.* Louisville, KY: American Printing House for the Blind.

Connolly, A., Nachtman, W., & Pritchett, E. M. (1976). *KeyMath Diagnostic Arithmetic Test.* Circle Pines, MN: American Guidance Service.

Croft, N.B., & Robinson, L.W. (1984). *Growing Up: A Developmental Curriculum.* Austin, TX: Parent Consultants.

Cruickshank, W. (Ed.). (1980). *Psychology of exceptional children and youth*. Englewood Cliffs, NJ: Prentice-Hall.

Davis, C. (1980). *Perkins-Binet Test of Intelligence for the Blind*. Watertown, MA: Perkins School for the Blind.

Dolch, E. (1955). *Methods in reading*. Champaign, IL: Garrard.

Dunst, C. (1982). The clinical utility of Piagetian-based scales of infant development. *Infant Mental Health Journal, 3,* 259–275.

Dunst, C. (1980). *A clinical and educational manual for use with the Uzgiris and Hunt Scales of Infant Psychological Development*. Austin, TX: PRO-ED.

Fagan, J. F. (1982). New evidence for the prediction of intelligence from infancy. *Infant Mental Health Journal, 3,* 219–228.

Fewell, R. R. (1983). New directions in the assessment of young handicapped children. In C. E. Reynolds & J. H. Clark (Eds.), *Assessment and programming for young children with low-incidence handicaps* (pp. 1-41). New York: Plenum Press.

Fry, E. (1980). The new instant word list. *The Reading Teacher, 34.* 284.

Gelfand, D. M., & Hartman, D. P. (1984). *Child behavior analysis and therapy* (2nd ed.). New York: Pergamon Press.

Gilbert, J., & Rubin, E. (1965). Evaluating the intellect of blind children. *The New Outlook for the Blind, 59,* 238–240.

Goldman, F. H., & Duda, D. (1978). Psychological assessment of the visually impaired child. In R. K. Mulliken & M. Evans (Eds.), *Assessment of children with low-incidence handicaps*. Stratford, CT.: NASP Publications Office. (pp. 52–57).

Hall, V. (1983). *The measurement of behavior* (rev. ed.). Austin, TX: PRO-ED.

Hammill, D. D. (in press). *Assessing the abilities and instructional needs of students*. Austin, Texas: PRO-ED.

Hammill, D. D. (1985). *Detroit Tests of Learning Aptitude*. Austin, TX: PRO-ED.

Hammill, D. D., & Leigh, J. E. (1983). *Basic School Skills Inventory–Diagnostic*. Austin, TX: PRO-ED.

Hammill, D. D., & Newcomer, P. L. (1982). *Test of Language Development–Intermediate*. Austin, TX: PRO-ED.

Hammill, D. D., Brown, V., Larsen, S., & Wiederholt, J. L. (1980). *Test of Adolescent Language*. Austin, TX: PRO-ED.

Hayes, S. (1942). Alternative scales for the mental measurement of the visually handicapped. *Outlook for the Blind, 4,* 225–250.

Higgins, L. C. (1973). *Classification in the congenitally blind*. New York: American Foundation for the Blind.

Hopkins, K. D., & McGuire, L. (1966). The validity of the Wechsler Intelligence Scale for Children. *The International Journal for the Education of the Blind, 15* 65–73.

Jastak, J., & Jastak, S. (1984). *Wide Range Achievement Test*. Wilmington, DE: Jastak Associates.

Kederis, C. J., Nolan, C. Y., & Morris, J. E. (1967). The use of controlled exposure devices to increase braille reading rates. *The Education of the Blind, May,* 97–105.

Korch, B. M., Gozzi, E. K., & Frances, V. (1968). Gaps in doctor-patient communication: Doctor-patient interaction and parent satisfaction. *Pediatrics, 42,* 855–871.

Lesiak, J., & Bradley-Johnson, S. (1983). *Reading assessment for placement and programming.* Springfield, IL: Charles C Thomas.

Madden, R., Gardner, E. R., Rudman, H. C., Karlson, B., & Merwin, J. C. (1973). *Stanford Achievement Test.* New York: Harcourt Brace Jovanovich.

Markland, M. H. (1979). *Assessing kindergarten children with Project Vision Up: A cognitive study using selected standardized measurements.* Unpublished doctoral dissertation, Brigham Young University, Provo, UT.

Maxfield, K. E., & Buchholz, S. (1957). *A Social Maturity Scale for Blind Preschool Children.* New York: American Foundation for the Blind.

Newborg, J., Stock, J. R., Wnek, L., Guidubaldi, J., & Svinicki, J. (1984). *Battelle Developmental Inventory.* Allen, TX: DLM/Teaching Resources.

Newcomer, P. L., & Hammill, D. D. (1982). *Test of Language Development–Primary.* Austin, TX: PRO-ED.

Newland, T. E. (1971). *Blind Learning Aptitude Test.* Champaign, IL: University of Illinois Press.

Ozias, D. K. (1975). Achievement assessment of the visually handicapped. *Education of the Visually Handicapped, 8,* 76–84.

Piaget, J. (1952). *The origins of intelligence in children* (M. Cook, Trans.). New York: International Universities Press.

Public Law 94–142. (1975). Washington, DC: Educational Amendments.

Public Law 93–112. (1971, May 4). Section 504 *Federal Registrar* 22676-22692. (121 a. 532).

Ross, A. (1976). *Psychological aspects of learning disabilities and reading disorders.* New York: McGraw-Hill.

Salvia, J., & Ysseldyke, J. E. (1981). *Assessment in special and remedial education.* Boston: Houghton Mifflin.

Scholl, G.T. (1983). Assessing the visually impaired child. In S. Ray, M. J. O'Neill, & N. T. Morris (Eds.), *Low incidence children: A guide to psychoeducational assessment* (pp. 67–90). Natchitoches, LA: Steven Ray.

Scholl, G. T., & Schnur, R. (1975). Measures of psychological, vocational, and educational functioning in the blind and visually handicapped: Introductory remarks. *The New Outlook,* October, 365–370.

Scott, E. P., Jan, J. E., & Freeman, R. D. (1985). *Can't your child see?* Austin, TX: PRO-ED.

Sparrow, S., Balla, D., & Cicchetti, D. V. (1984). *Vineland Adaptive Behaviol Scales–Expanded Form.* Circle Pines, MN: American Guidance Service.

Swallow, R., Mangold, S., & Mangold, P. (1978). *Informal Assessment of Developmental Skills for Visually Handicapped Students.* New York: American Foundation for the Blind.

Thorndike, R. L., Hagen, E. P., & Sattler, J. M. (1986). *Stanford-Binet Intelligence Scale: Fourth Edition.* Chicago, IL: Riverside.

Tillman, M. H. (1973). Intelligence scales for the blind: A review with implications for research. *Journal of School Psychology, 11,* 80–87.

Tillman, M. H., & Osborne, R. T. (1969). The performance of blind and sighted children on the Wechsler Intelligence Scale for Children: Interaction effects. *Education of the Visually Handicapped, 1,* 1–4.

Tillman, M. H. (1967). The performance of blind and sighted children on the Wechsler Intelligence Scale for Children: Study 1. *The Education of the Blind,* March, 65–74.

Uzgiris, I., & Hunt, J. (1975). *Ordinal Scales of Psychological Development.* Urbana, IL: University of Illinois Press.

Vander Kolk, C. J. (1981). *Assessment and planning with the visually impaired.* Austin, TX: PRO-ED.

Wechsler, D. (1981). *Wechsler Adult Intelligence Scale-Revised.* San Antonio: The Psychological Corporation.

Wechsler, D. (1974). *Wechsler Intelligence Scale for Children–Revised.* San Antonio: The Psychological Corporation.

Wechsler, D. (1967). *Wechsler Preschool and Primary Scale of Intelligence.* San Antonio: The Psychological Corporation.

Wright, F. J. (1980). *Project Vision Up assessment: Validity and reliability.* Unpublished doctoral dissertation. Brigham Young University, Provo, Utah.

Index